A MEMOIR OF SURVIVAL AND FORGIVENESS

TRAVELING
THE
ROAD
OF
SOLITUDE

RINA LIV, APRN

FLOWER *of* LIFE PRESS

"*I am lucky enough to work with Rina Liv and witness her love for others.* Traveling the Path of Solitude: A Memoir of Survival and Forgiveness *will motivate anyone who desires to improve their life. Rina's brutal honesty shows us that if she can make it through her difficult childhood and come out the other side as caring as she is, then* anyone *can follow in her footsteps. This book will help others cope with their life tragedies so they can find hope for the future.*"

—Rhonda Woodside APRN; Adult Nurse Practitioner

"*Rina's ability to be completely vulnerable and open about her painful past is phenomenal. Her self-discovery journey and her path to experiencing unconditional love through her relationship with God and her children are nothing short of inspiring. Her story has encouraged and helped me to open and evaluate some hidden and painful memories of my own. Rina shows us how important it is to heal and regain the ultimate power that God has given every one of us. Through God, all things are possible, and we, too, can live happier and healthier lives because of it.*"

—Briana Mussaw, The Reader's Compass, International Book Reviewers

"Traveling the Path of Solitude: A Memoir of Survival and Forgiveness *is the inspiring story of the power of faith to overcome overwhelming hardships from a lifetime of abuse. Rina's strength in overcoming the scars from her past comes from her never-wavering faith in God. Her life's journey has allowed her to become the successful woman she is today—a beacon of light with a beautiful soul and a heart warm enough to melt any attempt to freeze her spirit. This is a story of incredible resiliency in defying all those who endeavored to bring her down. It's a story of hope for the broken in soul and spirit and a powerful example of finding strength through inner reflection and faith."*

—SoPaul Moos

"It's hard to believe how much trauma and pain was hiding inside this strong and amazing woman. Despite all she's been through, she never lacked respect, empathy, or care for any other person in need. I hope that her journey of self-love and reflection in this book inspires and heals others. This book is proof of what I've witnessed in our long-term friendship and goes to show that even when all the odds are against you, you can still come out on top and remain humble."

—Ewa Rozek

"The first time I met Rina, I thought, 'Who is this outgoing character with so much energy?' She was always positive and willing to help anyone—with a smile. As I got to know her through her work in medicine, I became more intrigued by her light and freedom. Reading this book and understanding her back story and triumphs over adversity just amaze me. I am truly grateful to know someone so remarkable. I hope you too find Traveling the Path of Solitude: A Memoir of Survival and Forgiveness *just as impressive."*

—Lindsay McGinnis, NP

FLOWER *of* LIFE PRESS

Traveling the Road of Solitude: A Memoir of Survival and Forgiveness
By Rina Liv

The content of this book is for general instruction only. Each person's physical, emotional, and spiritual condition is unique. The instruction in this book is not intended to replace or interrupt the reader's relationship with a physician or other mental health professional. Please consult your doctor for matters pertaining to your specific health.

Cover and Book design by Astara Jane Ashley,
www.floweroflifepress.com

Published by Flower of Life Press
Old Saybrook, CT.
Visit us at www.floweroflifepress.com

Download your FREE GIFT from Flower of Life Press:
www.bestsellerpriestess.com/bestseller-priestess

Library of Congress Control Number: Available Upon Request

ISBN-13: 978-1-7349730-6-8

Printed in the United States of America

DEDICATION

I dedicate this book to my two oldest daughters Somonthearvy and Mary Sovan. I see myself in them when I was their age. They both have an independent and fighting spirit as I did, not wanting to rely on others and only relying on themselves. They are also ambitious, kind, and compassionate, always wanting to help others who are less fortunate and with a desire to give back. I wrote this book hoping to inspire them and let them know that despite everything I went through, I overcame it all by the grace of God. I want them to know that when everyone else around them fails them, never lose hope or faith. To standfast by God and He will be the light that guides them through their darkest hours—as He did with me.

I also dedicate this book to my niece and my four nephews, who taught me to open my heart to them. When I thought I had no one, they were there, loving me for me. I love their innocence—an innocence that I never had. Their hearts are pure, loving, and kind. I pray that God will always protect them and keep their hearts pure. I pray that God will make Himself known to them and give them the desire to seek Him, as He has with me.

Finally, I dedicate this book to my two godsons, Joseph and Nathan Alarcon, who taught me that I could be a great mother despite my upbringing, doubts, and insecurities (Joseph has been testing and pushing me to the limit ever since he was a toddler.) Through them, I've learned to be patient, protective, forgiving, and loving. They will always have a special place in my heart.

Contents

Introduction

My life journey starts at the age of forty-eight years old. For many decades, I have repressed deeply painful memories. I am now facing these painful memories and moving on with my life. It is my job to heal—no one can do it for me, so here I am.

But where do I begin? Am I even ready to deal with those painful memories? I can see that I am heading toward self-destruction if I do not deal with it now, which is why I am sharing my story—to aid in the process of my healing and inspire others in their healing journey.

Sometimes I wonder what my life would be like if I had a "normal" childhood, but then I remember that all the struggles I endured at an early age made me who I am today: a strong, compassionate, independent woman who loves life.

It has been a long, arduous journey, and it took me until my late forties to finally get here. But here I am—still standing.

❦

My abuse started when I was a baby by my step-grandmother. I thought my abuse would have ended after escaping from Cambodia and my step grandmother's wrath, but I was wrong.

My dad, mother, step-grandfather, two brothers, and I came to the United States in the Winter of 1975. We were poor immigrants displaced from our home country because of the war. We went to the United States with nothing and didn't even speak the language. My father worked hard to provide for us and to make a life for his family. He was the only positive role model that I had growing up.

At the age of five, my mother started abusing me physically, mentally, and emotionally. I was told I was nothing and that I would amount to nothing. Not only did I endure my mother's abuse, but also sexual abuse at the hands of my step-grandfather.

I had always lived a sheltered life. My mother had always controlled me and who I could have as friends. I was sheltered from Western cultures, and I could not have friends outside our Cambodian community. At the age of eighteen, I joined the Army to escape from my mother's control. Being exposed to Western culture was a rude awakening for me. I was naive and had so much to learn. I was living in the United States, but I was raised with traditional Cambodian beliefs. I felt lost between two cultures. I didn't fit in and didn't feel like I belonged to either of them.

Somehow, I have learned who I am and have woven the two cultures together. I came out of the Army with a healthier mind but still confused about who I was as a person. At that time, I was not aware of how my childhood sexual abuse had negatively affected my relationships with men. I still had a lot of learning and growing to do to fully blossom into who I wanted to be as a person.

I assessed myself on what needed to be healed. God was always faithful and never abandoned me even though, at times, I felt abandoned by Him. He had worked on me, molded me, taught me to love, have faith, be patient, be compassionate, and be non-judgmental towards myself and others.

God gave me a softness and an open heart. However, getting to that place required intense excavating through the dirt of my guilt and shame.

But now, I have a voice, and I choose not to suffer anymore.

If you are suffering in any way, dear reader, my wish is that this book open your heart and fill it with hope and the knowing that you are *never* alone.

~Rina

Lost and Found

Sometimes I feel that I was born to be lost. I am a mystery even to myself. I do not know my birth father, the month or day of my birth, or the city where I was born.

All I know is that I was born in Cambodia in 1970, the year of the dog. While most Cambodians were victims of genocide and war crimes during that time, I was a victim of abuse by those closest to me.

I have repressed many painful memories for nearly five decades and hidden my childhood trauma out of shame and not wanting anyone's pity. I've tried to move forward with my life.

So why now must I face these memories? Where do I even begin? Am I ready to deal with the pain and shame so deeply infused into my being and my memories? I see that I am heading toward destruction if I don't deal with it.

I want to be loved unconditionally and have a special someone in my life who loves me for who I am. But I question if people are even capable of loving unconditionally! Sometimes we grab onto any love just to fill the void and the emptiness in our lives, only to find that the love we caught is toxic. At least it was in my case.

My soul seeks real love, so I share my story hoping that it will inspire you, too, to discover where love really lives—inside of your own heart.

INCENSE

My abuse started early. When I look down at my belly, I see the childhood incense burn marks as my life battle wounds and scars. As a child, I never thought much of it, but as I grew up and saw other girls in the school gym with flawless bodies, I realized those marks weren't normal.

When I asked my mother about it, she told me that the incense burn marks happened when I was a baby. I couldn't understand it. Why would *anyone* burn a baby's stomach? I kept asking my mother questions until she finally told me: She would leave me with my step-grandmother while she was out working in the rice fields. My step-grandmother hated my mother so furiously that she directed that hate toward me, burning my stomach with incense so that every time my mother would look at it, she would feel the depth of how much she was hated.

My mother said she would come home and hear me cry— the cry of a child in pain. She would hold me and see burn marks on me. She didn't have a choice but to leave me with my step-grandmother, she says—and so the abuse continued.

My feelings toward my mother were already mixed, and now confusion and anger were added to the mix. I couldn't understand it. *How could she have left me, a helpless baby, with someone who would continue to burn me day after day? How long did this go on?*

For a long time, every time I looked at my scarred belly, I was reminded of that abuse and of my mother's inability to protect and defend me from a scornful and callous woman who thought that abusing someone's baby was the way to get back at her.

As an adult, I am sometimes ashamed of my imperfect body, scarred from years of abuse. I find myself hiding my scars, my pain, and my shame.

In my late twenties, I saw a cosmetic surgeon who I hoped could erase the scars from my belly so that I would no longer have to see them and be reminded of the abuse. But I was told that the scars were too deep and that the best he could do was laser it to make it lighter.

Even though she passed away a few years ago, I can still feel my mother's anger. My body and energy still feel like she is sneaking up behind me to beat me.

When I was five years old, she told me that she should have just thrown me off the ship while on our way to America. She continued to say this to me again and again.

I was always afraid of her—afraid of making her angry with me.

My father served in the Cambodia Marines when U.S. troops pulled out of Southeast Asia in 1973, and he knew the war would worsen without the protection from U.S. troops. He tried to get us out of Cambodia.

We would go into hiding during the day and only try to escape out of Cambodia at night.

Much later, I noticed that I had what looked like little indented spots all over my legs, so I asked my mother about them. She said that when we were escaping from Cambodia to Thailand, we would walk along the ocean shoreline at night to try to get into Thailand. We spent weeks in the ocean, and the saltwater had absorbed into my legs and made little dents or holes on my legs.

We had somehow managed to get to Thailand and then made it to the Philippines, where we stayed at a refugee camp. From there, a Baptist church sponsored us to come to the United States among the first wave of Southeast Asian immigrants in 1975. Once we got to America, we stayed at the refugee camp in Camp Pendleton, California, until our paperwork was completed and all immunizations were all up to date.

After U.S. troops left, my mother stayed in Phnom Penh with my father, and I was left with my nursemaid in the country. The war was heating up, so the nursemaid brought me to Phnom Penh, looking for my mother to give me back. But my mother didn't want me and was angry with the nursemaid. My father insisted that she take me. My mother has since admitted if he hadn't pressed, she would have left me to die. Suspecting that my mother had told me this story out of anger, I asked my father... and he confirmed it.

Based on the number of times she said she wanted to throw me overboard, I suspect that I was a painful reminder of something terrible that happened to her.

Every time I brought a report card home, my mother would tell me that I could do better—or that I would never amount to anything. Either way, I was never good enough for her. I promised myself that I would never let her see that she got the best of me. Whatever I set out to do, I always made sure I succeeded. I needed to prove my mother wrong.

When I was in my late twenties, I asked her why she treated me so badly when I was a child. She cried and said I was making up stories, and then accused me of lying about how she had treated me.

I walked away and never asked her again.

I won't ever know why. And I have let it go.

Traveling the Road of Solitude

You Deserve a Break Today

We came by ship to the United States in the winter of 1975 and stayed at the immigration camp at Camp Pendleton. We were not allowed to leave the camp until we had all our papers and immunizations and had a sponsor. Our first sponsor was from Colorado. At that time, many members of churches sponsored Cambodians. We went to Colorado. I remember there was lots of snow, and it was freezing. We were from a place where it was always hot and humid, and my father did not like snow. But we had no money and had no place to go.

Our sponsor owned a hotel in the mountains in Colorado. My mother would clean the hotel rooms, and guests would leave tips for her, but she didn't know that the tip money was meant for her, so she gave it all to our sponsor. My father worked as a handyman, fixing things that were broken on the property. My step-grandfather worked as the groundskeeper, picking up trash and keeping the hotel grounds clean.

Our sponsor did not pay my parents or my step-grandfather for their labor. They were basically working for food and shelter. Our sponsor took the money plus any other aid that was given to our family. We didn't see a penny. We all lived in one hotel room and were allowed in our sponsor's house for three meals per day, with nothing between meals.

My father saw that we could not live like this, not having anything and practically working for free. He was very good at mechanics and fixing things. Every time a car would break down, he would see this as an opportunity to make some money and hide it from our sponsor. He fixed cars that were stranded and broken down near the hotel, and people would pay him. He saved that money, and in about six months, he had saved enough to get us back to Camp Pendleton on a bus. Our sponsor did not want us to leave, but my father, with his very limited English, insisted that they get us a bus fare with the money he had saved up. Our sponsor was shocked because he had assumed we had no money. My father did not back down until they finally took us to the bus station, where we bought our fares back to Camp Pendleton.

On the way back to Camp Pendleton, the bus stopped at McDonald's. We didn't speak or read English, and it was our first-time ordering food at a restaurant in a foreign country. We didn't know what we were ordering, so we pointed at what looked good. My dad took our tray and went to sit down without paying for our food. We didn't know that we were supposed to pay when we got our food! In Cambodia, we didn't pay until we were finished eating, and we thought this rule also applied to the United States. We just sat down and ate, while people muttered words we couldn't understand and stared at us. After we finished eating, my father walked up to the cashier counter and paid.

Sometimes when I pass a McDonald's, I smile.

Hidden

I knew very little about my mother's past. All I had heard was that she was raised in a rural village, her father was the head villager, and she was spoiled when she was a child. She didn't like school, playing hooky and eventually, quitting. She was illiterate. She couldn't read or write the Khmer language, or English. Emotionally, too, it was as if she had not developed past the teenage phase. She would get upset and act out with a fury that didn't match the situation.

One day she was angry, grabbed a wire hanger, and started hitting me on the head with it. She had hit me a few times with the sharp edge of the hook, and I started bleeding.

When she saw that my head was bleeding, she stopped.

I went to my room and stayed away from her and out of her sight. This was the first of many times when I would hide from her.

Why did she stop? Maybe she was scared.

We had been in the United States for less than a year. Maybe she was afraid that she would get into trouble for beating me. Or maybe she felt remorse.

She kept me home from school that week, until the scab on my head healed.

She never hit me on the head again. Instead, she beat me on my back or legs, where my clothes would conveniently hide the bruises and scars.

DREAMS

As a girl, I had three reoccurring dreams over the course of many years. In one dream, I am locked in a white room with no doors. I feel the walls for a hidden door, but there is nothing. I am locked, trapped with nothing but empty space. I feel abandoned, as if I have no one in this world. I wake up from the dream crying, thinking I am still trapped in that room. And in a way, I am: I am totally alone.

In the second dream, I am sleeping, and when I wake up, everyone is gone. They have all left me. I look for my mother, dad, step-grandfather, and two brothers, but they are nowhere to be found. Again, when I wake up, I feel unwanted, abandoned, and alone.

In the third dream, my mother is angry and looking for me so she can beat me, but I hide and she can't find me. Finally, when darkness comes, I sneak out of the house and climb over the wall of the neighbor's yard until I find a bush to hide in so she can't see me. I hide in those bushes and don't dare move or make a sound, fearing discovery and being dragged back home. Then, when I wake up, I experience an overwhelming sense of fear and anxiety and do not know which reality I am in.

In school, I didn't felt accepted or that I fit in anywhere. I had friends, so I seemed happy and secure; no one would ever have suspected the abuse I endured at home. At an early age, I had learned to hide my feelings and my thoughts. I never showed any emotion. If I couldn't trust my mother or my step-grandfather, who were supposed to protect me yet abused me repeatedly, who could I trust? I kept myself walled in, protected but alone, never letting anyone get too close. I never wanted to get hurt again.

As a kid, I had a vivid imagination. I spent a great deal of time alone or hiding in the hallway closet behind the clothes for hours with nothing but my imagination to pass the time. I daydreamed of a better life and a loving mother, and in my imagination, I would travel all over the world. I would imagine my white horse, and I would ride on his back as we flew over the vast ocean.

The Darkness of Hatred

Hatred started early in my life. I hated my step-grandmother for leaving scars that are forever embedded in me, and I hated my mother for not protecting me when I couldn't defend myself.

I was her baby girl. Why didn't she care? How could she have abandoned me in this way? Why was I treated as useless and worthless?

My abuse didn't end there. It continued as repeating dysfunctional patterns and personal choices that perpetuated it. Looking back, I can see why: My soul *had* to become wounded so that I could heal myself and serve others in their healing journeys.

My heart grew cold and callous—it was the only way I knew how to survive. But even then, something in me knew that anger was not the answer.

My mother had secrets. When I asked about my biological father, she would either get upset with me or tell me inconsistent stories about him.

Her feelings and emotions were all over the place. She could be loving and caring at times, but mostly she was depressed and sad. She would take her anger and frustration out on me physically, emotionally, and mentally. When I was in my twenties, I tried to get close to her and have a more intimate mother-daughter relationship. But, somehow, I would end up feeling like I was nothing. She couldn't abuse me physically anymore, but the emotional and verbal abuse continued. When I was in grade school, I would hide in the closet when she came home from work because I didn't know what mood she would be in.

I still don't know anything about my biological father. Did she hate him, or did he do something awful to her, and every time she looks at me, she sees him? Is that why she hates me so much because I remind her of him and whatever he did to hurt her? She reminds me continually that I was unwanted. Sometimes I wonder whether he raped her and if I should have had more compassion toward her.

How can I ever let anyone into my heart when my heart is as cold and callous as my mother's?

$$\sim$$

I was eight or nine when I first felt hatred toward her. She was angry again for a reason I didn't understand, and she told me to go outside and pick a branch. I was strategic and chose the smallest one, thinking that it would break after she hit me with it a couple of times. But she kept hitting my back with that branch, and it never broke. Wanting to scream, I held back tears as close to silence as I could bear; I didn't want her to think that she got the best of me, which angered her even more. I thought she would beat me to death, but then her husband stepped in and stopped her. I cried all night, asking God, "What did I ever do to deserve such a mother?"

Please, God, either take her or take me.

That night, it felt like darkness filled my entire heart.

Standing Beside the Ocean

As a child, I knew that my life would be challenging and a long, painful journey. Today, as I close my eyes, I see that frightened little girl being swallowed up by her environment with thoughts of wanting to hide, run away, and escape. She was so trapped, so doomed. Where was she supposed to go?

I remember repeatedly dreaming of a white horse. I was in a cave and surrounded by the ocean—so calm and beautiful with its crystal blue color and vast endlessness. *Where does it end?* I wondered. *If I were to take a trip across that ocean, where would it take me?* The white horse would fly down from the heavens, spread its wings, and soar across the clear blue sky above the ocean so majestically. He would land beside me in the cave and comfort me. I would stroke his white mane while we stood together, gazing across the vast sea. Sometimes, he would let me ride on his back and we would fly over the ocean. In that world, I was free.

Despite all that I endured, my heart remained pure. Whenever I felt distressed and in despair, my white horse would find me in my dream and comfort me. But as I got older, he stopped showing up. Was it because my heart was growing cold and callous? When I imagined never seeing him again, I would feel anxious.

Maybe if I remind myself of that innocent little girl with her white horse, it will somehow feel the same...

Looking back at this dream now, I realize why I feel comforted every time I am near an ocean, lake, or river. It's as if the water calls out to me. I stand and listen to the ocean waves crashing, the river flowing, or the stream trickling, and I find comfort.

I want to walk into that comfort and swim in it. I imagine myself as a mermaid swimming in the wide-open ocean, free from all worries of the world, surrounded by the beautiful sea creatures that God has created.

I am beginning to feel that I am worth saving.

Dirty Little Secret

My most painful memory was when I was six, and we had been in the United States for about a year. That day is branded into my memory like a hot iron; I call it my *Scarlet Letter*. I was lying on the couch in the living room, taking a nap after school. The couch was where the window was, and I remember waking up from my nap as a dark figure pulled off my pants and laid on top of me. Once I was fully awake and my eyes adjusted, I realized it was my step-grandfather. I wasn't sure what he was doing to me, but I felt pain and confusion.

When he was done with me, he told me that this was our secret and that I could never tell anyone because my mother would be angry at me and I would get into trouble with her.

For years, I kept this dirty little secret.

My mother was an abuser, not a protector. She allowed this perverted old man to do with me as he pleased. I never quite understood what he was doing to me, but I knew it wasn't good. I knew that it was bad. So many times, I wanted to tell my mother what he was doing to me. When the family would take off without me, I begged to go with them, but my step-grandfather would tell my mother to go ahead and go and that he would watch me. The abuse went on until I was eleven.

I never told my mother.

At an early age, I learned that I had to protect myself and that nobody would protect me.

My mother would rent a room out to make extra money. One day, I overheard our housemate describing her sex life with her husband to one of her friends. I realized that this was what my step-grandfather was doing to me. It sounded so disgusting, and shame washed over me. I just wanted to bleach my entire body to get rid of the filth of that old man from me.

I went into my housemate's room and asked her if I told her something would she promise not to tell anyone, especially my mother. She promised. I told her what my step-grandfather did to me. She asked me if he was still doing that to me, and I told her, yes, since I was about five or six. She left the room and immediately told my mother. My mother came running in and asked if it was true. I only nodded because I was afraid she was going to beat me. She ran out of the room and started cursing and yelling at my step-grandfather. She kicked him out of the house and told him to never come back. I was so relieved because now he could never hurt me again.

But my mother thought of him as her father, and she missed him.

He was back within a month.

I felt so betrayed and hurt. How could my mother have let this predator, who molested her only daughter for years, come back home?

By now, I had lost all faith—especially with my mother. My stepdad didn't do anything to protect me either, because he was loyal to his father. When he heard all the commotion with my mother yelling when she found out, he just walked away.

My step-grandfather did move back home, but thankfully, he never touched me again after that incident.

I will forever wear that Scarlet Letter.

Later, I discovered that what he had done to me had left me barren and forever scarred. My mother's friends would gossip and say that I couldn't have children because I "played" with too many boys. Other people would ask me, "What is wrong with you? Why can't you have children?"

And I would just silently cry from the inside.

I didn't speak of my longing to be a mother or why I was barren. That was a deep, dark secret that I hid for decades. Every time a memory would come to the surface, I suppressed it. I was in denial for decades that it ever happened, until in my thirties, when all the memories, shame, and guilt resurfaced—against my will, but ultimately, for the health of my soul.

To Church

I close my eyes, and I become a seven-year-old girl playing outside on a warm Sunday morning.

Every Sunday morning, I see a young Caucasian family with a three-year-old daughter dressed up and getting in their car to go somewhere.

One morning I asked them where they were going.

"To church," the mother said. "Do you want to come with us?"

"Let me ask my mother," I said.

"What is church?" my mother asked.

"I don't know, but I want to go," I said.

I went to church with them almost every Sunday until they moved out of our apartment complex. Much later, I realized that this was the beginning of discovering the faith that had saved me from a life of self-destruction.

I don't remember much of what I felt when I first stepped into a church, but I do remember seeing many nicely-dressed Caucasian people.

My neighbor walked me to Sunday school, but I can't remember how I felt or what I did. Perhaps I heard the gospel but wasn't ready to understand it...

At home, because my parents were Buddhist, all I knew was Buddhism. Exposed to Buddhism and to Christianity, I felt that I don't know where I belonged, who or what I was.

One time, as a seven-year-old, I looked down at the Buddha statue at my friend's house and thought, "How can that be a God? He's fat. And if he is a God, why do people put him on the ground? Why not put him high on a shelf?"

Born in Cambodia, raised by Cambodian parents who held onto the traditional ways, and yet exposed to Western culture, I didn't quite know where I fit. I could have Caucasian friends at school but could never bring them home or go to their homes. At home, I was to speak only Cambodian and to have only Cambodian friends chosen by my mother, and there were few Cambodians to choose from in the late 1970s. For Christmas, we would put up a fake tree and go out for Chinese food. I was stuck between two cultures, not allowed to be myself or to choose for myself; it was all controlled by my mother.

THE AMERICAN DREAM

We had only been in the United States for three years when my father, a hard worker, had saved enough money to buy a house. That was 1978, and I was seven or eight. Money was tight for that first year, with a mortgage in addition to the other bills. Before the house, we went to a laundromat on weekends. But at the new home, my mother said that we couldn't afford the laundromat anymore and that it was my job to wash the family's clothes. Every Saturday morning, I would get up early and start washing everyone's clothes by hand, which would take a couple of hours, then hang them to dry. I did this for about a year before we finally could afford to buy a washer and dryer.

Whenever money was a little tight for that month's bills, we would make a Saturday trip to Las Vegas. I loved that drive. It was all desert and a vast expanse of nothingness. My brothers and I didn't have much growing up; no toys or board games. But, on those long drives, we would play games with our imagination. We would look at the clouds, talk about what shapes we saw in their puffy formations—elephants, angels, etc.—and try to see those clouds as the others saw them. We would imagine the sun or the moon following us, lighting the highway for us. Or we would look for different out-of-state license plates. The first person to see a car with an out-of-state plate would call out that state and pinch the siblings who didn't see it or call it out first. We would also play the "I see" game. As we drove by something, we would describe what we saw, and the others would guess what it was.

In Las Vegas, our parents would either go to Circus-Circus or the Strip. When we arrived, they would leave us kids to entertain ourselves. If we were at Circus-Circus, we would walk around the casino and people watch, or we would play games with a roll of quarters until we ran out of money. When we got tired, we would sit on the floor in the corner of the hotel's front entrance waiting for our parents to come back.

If we went to the Strip, my brothers and I would walk around. People would leave their cocktail or beer glasses along the edges outside of the casino windows, so we would collect as many as we could carry and take them home with us. Let's just say, our house did *not* have a shortage of glasses.

When our parents would find us at the end of the night, I could tell everything by the look on my mother's face. If she looked happy, they had won, and we would exit the freeway to stop for Chinese food, and everyone could order what they wanted. But if she didn't look happy, the drive back home was silent. We didn't dare upset her any more than she already was. Their loss meant we would have to live tight for that month.

Luckily, there were more wins than losses.

CHINESE JUMP ROPE

As a kid, I loved to play Chinese jump rope with the girls at school. We would start at ankle height, and if you could jump over it, the elastic would be moved higher and higher. One Saturday when I was in third grade, I tied a rope— not a rubber band—to a tree at home and played the game by myself, moving the rope higher and higher every time I made the jump. When the rope was at shoulder height, I made the jump. But the rope didn't move like the ones made from the rubber bands, and I fell, my left arm landing hard on a tree root. The pain was intense, but I hid it because I was afraid my mother would give me a beating for doing something so stupid.

The next morning, my mother asked me to go to the store and pick up some ingredients. I got on my bike and tried to ride it with one hand, but I knew I couldn't carry that bag of groceries back with my left hand. And, no matter what the consequences, I couldn't hide the pain anymore. I told her what had happened, and to my surprise, she was worried about me. She and my step-grandfather thought maybe I had dislocated my left shoulder, so they tried to pull it back into place, which made the pain worse. She took me to the emergency room, where they said the arm was broken and they put a cast on it.

That evening, my mother and my step-grandfather chopped down those two big trees. Was that protective act a glimpse of my mother's love for me? Did she truly love me somewhere deep down in her heart? I was confused.

SOCIAL SECURITY

When I was in the seventh grade, my mother had a seizure at work, was taken to the hospital, and was diagnosed with a brain tumor. At that time, during the early 1980s, hospitals were not required to have a certified interpreter, and it was a great deal of pressure on me as a twelve-year-old to be the interpreter for my parents. I didn't know any of the medical terminologies in either language.

Dear God, I prayed. *I only want to be a child. Why can't you just let me be a child?* Through it all, God was the one thing that I was sure of. I had no one, so I clung to God to keep from going off the deep end. He was always looking out for me and bringing the person who I needed most into my life at that time. God had sent the ocean, the cave, and my white horse in my dreams when I most needed them, to comfort me and let me know that I wasn't alone. I knew He was with me always.

My mother had surgery to remove her brain tumor. We didn't know if she would make it. I felt so guilty because when I was little, I had imagined my life would be better without her and so prayed for God to either take me or take her. Had God chosen to take her now?

I prayed, *Please, God save her.* To see her in such a fragile state broke my heart. How could I wish her dead? What kind of daughter was I to wish her mother dead? I would pray for forgiveness and that God would give me the heart to forgive her and to love her. I thought maybe the brain tumor explained why she was so mean to me. Perhaps she had no control over her actions or her emotions.

The neurosurgeon told us that her surgery went well but that she might still have some seizure activity and would be on two anti-seizure medications for life. Her emotional instability increased. Meanwhile, I had to interpret for her at medical appointments.

One day I went with her to apply for her permanent disability benefit, and I struggled to interpret Social Security questions in Cambodian. She started crying and telling the lady that I was no good and could never help her. She had abused me only in private before then, but now, she had beat me in public. When my stepfather drove us home from the Social Security office, my mother told him to pull over, and she ordered me to get out of the car. He tried to rationalize with her, but I gladly got out of the car, relieved to be kicked out rather than beaten.

As I walked home, I prayed, *Dear God, do I go back home? Or is this my chance to run away? But where would I go?*

I took my time walking home, wondering if I would be beaten when I got there. I did not want to live anymore.

I often sat in the dark, alone, helpless, and hopeless with my wild thoughts running ahead of me. I asked God, *"What are your plans for me? Will I forever suffer in silence? Am I made to be abused? Will I ever have peace and love in my heart?"*

I sat alone on the cold bathroom floor with a knife in my hand. *Will this be the day?* I pleaded to God, asking Him to please get me out of this horrible place.

All I ever wanted was a mother to love—and for her to love me back.

PIGGY BANK

I was in third grade when we did a Christmas gift exchange. I felt all the presents and picked the heaviest one, thinking that it will be a good gift in there. I opened it up, and it was a glass piggy bank. I remember just loving that gift. That was the best present I had ever received. One girl in my class asked if I would exchange it with her because she had bought it for her friend to pick—that gift was meant for her and nobody else. I refused to give it to her. I thought, "They will always get beautiful presents from their friends and families, while I will *maybe* get clothes... or nothing at all. I felt badly for not giving it to her, yet I was so happy that I would finally have somewhere to store my coins.

I cherished that glass piggy bank for years. Then one morning, when I was twelve, while outside in the front yard, my mother got angry at me for some reason. She went to my room, grabbed my glass piggy bank, brought it outside, and threw it against the concrete wall between our house and our neighbor's house. Glass shattered everywhere, and my coins spilled out, rolling away. I loved that bank, and, at that moment, I hated her with a passion.

Even as a young adult, I kept looking for the same bank. Somehow, I believed that if I had it, everything would be alright.

Sweet Sixteen

We never really celebrated birthdays, but the year I turned sixteen, a friend asked if we could celebrate at my house. I told her I would ask my mother. I was scared to ask, but I'd never had a birthday party before, and I wanted one. To my surprise, she agreed and let me have a birthday party at our house.

I was so excited to finally be like a regular teenage girl and have friends over. My friend came over and helped me decorate the garage. She and her mother had cooked and brought food, and my mother had bought a birthday cake. My friend invited a lot of her Cambodian friends, including boys. I was afraid of my mother's reaction because I was not allowed to befriend any boys. To my surprise, she was okay with it, because they were not *my* friends.

"This is going to be the best first birthday ever!" I thought. But my step-grandfather started drinking when my friend showed up, and he was drunk by the time the party started. He didn't like it at all when the boys started showing up. He kept coming into the garage, yelling at the guys, telling them to get out. It was so embarrassing. My mother tried but couldn't contain his belligerent behavior. He kept yelling at everyone to get out, and eventually, they did.

My face was red with shame and embarrassment. That's when I realized that I needed to leave that house to save myself. I had to leave so I could live my own life, free from this nightmare and abuse. But I knew I couldn't run away from home; if I did, the authorities or my school would make me come back. I never wanted to come back to this house.

My first birthday party was a disaster. It was a decade or so after that before I ever celebrated another birthday.

∿

I was sixteen when the physical abuse stopped. But the verbal, mental, and emotional abuse continued until the day my mother died.

I was mostly not allowed to have any friends over, but my closest friend did occasionally visit. My mother didn't like her because she was African American, and she would accuse her of stealing something whenever she would leave.

My friend was not a thief.

My mother was forgetful, and her "stolen items" always turned up where she'd left them.

One day, my girlfriend and I were both in the kitchen. My mother saw her and got angry for no reason. She started yelling at me in Cambodian, and my girlfriend gave me a look that asked, "What is wrong with her?" Embarrassed by the outburst, I suggested that we go. I got up and walked to the kitchen sink to put away our water glasses when I heard my friend yell, "Duck!" Thankfully, I followed my instinct and ducked low just as my mother threw a glass at me. The glass hit the kitchen cabinet and shattered. It would have hit my back just like it had with my father. I knew never to turn my back on her, but I was naive in thinking that she wouldn't hurt me in front of someone else. I was wrong.

Anger overcame me. I was not about to take her abuse anymore. Angry that she had missed me, she ran to me and put out her hand to strike me. I caught her wrist, squeezed it, and told her that if she ever laid a hand on me again, I would kill her. *Would* I have killed her? Looking back now, I don't know. But I thank God that I wasn't put in that position again for another year.

Not His Daughter

I was twelve when I found out that my father was actually my stepfather, not my biological father. I was devastated. It would have been easier to believe that my mother wasn't my real mother than to believe my father wasn't my real father.

That day my mother was angry about something, and I was in sight and her target as usual. She yelled at me and then started hitting me. Stubborn, I refused to cry. I would never let that woman ever see that she had gotten the best of me. My father stepped in and tried to stop her from beating me. She yelled at him and said that I was not his daughter, for him to butt out and that she could treat me however she wanted to because I was her daughter and not his.

My thoughts were spinning. *What? Did I hear that right? Did she just say that I was not his daughter?*

I started yelling at her, not caring what she did to me. She had given birth to me. She controlled my life. She told me time and again that I would amount to nothing. But I didn't look to her as a mother. I had always been obedient and well-behaved, doing whatever she asked of me without complaint. But now I demanded the truth from her.

"Is he my father?"

She just walked away like a coward.

I looked at my father—the man I had known as my father—and saw the pain in his eyes.

I asked him if he was my dad.

He shook his head and told me no. I asked him if he knew who my birth father was, and again he shook his and told me no that he did not know who my father was, and he walked away, too.

I was truly alone, and I had to protect myself from her.

I wondered if she treated me differently from my brothers because of who my father was... and now I had discovered that they were my half-brothers...What other lies or secrets was I unaware of? I was confused and hurt.

How could my biological father leave me with her? Why did he walk away from me? Would my life have been different if he had been around? Would she be a better person if he had been with us? I have no memories of him. Deep down, I never wanted to know him or meet him. He was as dead to me as she was. Neither of my biological parents wanted me, and one of them got stuck with me. I suspect that when she saw me, she was reminded of him, and she would take her hatred of him out on me. Just like my step-grandmother would take her hatred of my mother out on me.

CLAMMING

My youngest brother would do things that would scare any parents. I think he had used up all his "nine lives" when he was a little toddler. He was such a cute little chubby baby. When he was a baby, we lived in an apartment. One morning, we all went for a walk with my baby brother in a stroller. While my parents were looking at items at a garage sale, a car backed out of the long driveway and hit the stroller with my baby brother in it. My parents yelled at the car to stop, and luckily my little brother was okay. The driver told my parents that he would buy a stroller to replace the one he had hit, but he never returned.

We were poor and would go clamming, fishing, or go on a grunion run when in season. Grunion are fish that we could easily catch to feed the family for months. When my brother was three, we went to the grunion run, and my parents left him in the car with the keys in the ignition. Everyone was busy catching grunions when we suddenly saw the car heading out toward the ocean with my little brother in the driver's seat behind the wheel! My dad and our friends ran after the car to stop it from going into the ocean. Luckily, they stopped it!

My parents were close with my best childhood friends' parents, and we would go and do a lot of things together. When my little brother was about four, we went to Santa Barbara. We were clamming and just happened to see the Parks and Recreational authority. Our parents immediately dumped their clams, but my little brother had a small bucket and wouldn't dump it. The Parks and Recreational authorities walked over to my little brother and asked him what was in his bucket and, of course, he showed them. He was proud of all those clams! My parents got a $500 fine for clamming. We were poor, and that was a lot of money, but friends helped pay for half of it. We never went to Santa Barbara after that.

I had never seen my father abuse my mother no matter how she treated him, except for one time when we were clamming. I don't remember where. Everyone was busily clamming, and no one was watching my little brother, who had just barely learned to walk and was playing by the water. Then, all of a sudden, he fell in the water. My dad just happened to be looking in the direction my little brother was playing, but he didn't see him. Everyone was panicking because he was gone. My dad ran over to where he was playing and saw him in the water. He pulled my brother out of the water, and, thank God, he was okay. My dad walked over to where my mother was and slapped her hard on the face for not watching my brother. That was the only time I ever saw my dad hit my mother. We could have lost my little brother on that day, but God was watching over him.

A Father's Love

My father was a quiet man. He raised me when I was a baby, treated me as if I was his own daughter, never laid a hand on me, and tried to protect me from my mother as best as he could. He was the only role model I had growing up. He worked hard to provide for us, taking on two full-time jobs after my mother's surgery. While he was at work, I would hide because I knew there wouldn't be anyone to save me from her.

His life was problematic from the start. His mother had passed away when he was a baby, and his father raised him— and abused him. He ran away from home when he was eight or nine and took refuge at the Buddhist temple where he was raised by Buddhist monks. He made a vow to himself that he would never abuse children, including his own.

He also regularly endured verbal and physical abuse from my mother, but she would twist the story around and tell people that he was abusive with her. I knew better. I was there. I was seven when I first saw her physically abuse him. I had been her target, and when he tried to protect me, she turned her anger onto him. He walked away toward the back yard, and she grabbed a glass and threw it at his back. The glass shattered, and he just kept on walking into the garage. We both knew it was best to keep silent and walk away so we wouldn't fuel her anger even more.

He worked so much he was rarely home. One day we got a phone call from the hospital. He had fallen asleep behind the wheel and drove the car into a ditch off the side of the freeway. That day, I realized my mother was genuinely evil. Instead of caring about him, she said that he deserved it and hoped that he would die. At that moment, I was scared to death that I would be left alone with her. But miraculously, he was okay. *Thank you, God, for saving my father.*

When I was sixteen and got my driver's license, my dad bought me a used car that he had fixed up so I wouldn't have to walk to school anymore. I had to be at school too early to catch the school bus, so I had been walking a few miles each way. When I first started driving, he would get up early and wait outside my car door to make sure I put on my seatbelt. He wouldn't leave until I had it on. He never wore a seat belt when he was driving, but he always made sure I had mine on for the first couple of months when I started driving until it became a habit for me. I never start the engine of my car until my seatbelt is on as if he is still there, making sure I am safe.

My dad taught me to change my oil and to change my tires. He never wanted me to get stuck anywhere or rely on any man to take care of me. If I ever had a flat tire, he knew I would be okay and would be able to change it myself. No matter what I went through, I always had that independent spirit and the will to survive. I learned those traits from him.

What Happens in Vegas

When money was a little tight, we made the Las Vegas trip hoping that my parents would win a little bit to help pay for the month's bills. I had just barely gotten my driver's license when my father gave me the keys to the car and told me it was my turn to drive the family to Las Vegas. I was scared. That was a long way for a new driver like me, and I didn't even know how to get there! But he insisted that I drive. "How else will you learn?" he asked. And he would be there in the car with me so that nothing would happen.

After that, I drove them to Las Vegas many times. He trusted me to drive and to get us all safely there and back home. Everyone slept on the drive home, so there I was driving in the dark, essentially alone.

And I was fine.

To this day, driving never scares me. I would drive alone in the dark, on country roads, or in the rain, snow, or even ice. When I get stressed, going out for a beautiful scenic drive always seems to soothe my soul.

When I eventually left and wasn't there to absorb her anger, she turned it all on him.

Once I came back home, she told me that her husband had put her in an institution. Rather than believe her, I asked him. He showed me his left thigh, where she had stabbed him in a fit of rage. He had called the paramedics because he couldn't stop the bleeding, and they arrested her. He didn't press charges, so they let her out of jail.

I was twenty-eight when he finally divorced her, and she didn't go peacefully. She already had another lover and lived with him, but she would still come over and cause problems. I asked him why he hadn't divorced her a long time ago, and he said that he stayed because of me. He knew that if he ever left, she would kill me. And he also wanted to make sure that my two brothers would never endure what we had gone through.

I asked him why hadn't he told me earlier that he wasn't my biological father, and he replied that he was afraid that I wouldn't want to be his daughter anymore. He had watched me suffer and could do nothing to save me but stay in a loveless marriage to make sure she wouldn't kill me. He loved me as his own daughter.

Brothers

I left to join the Army when my brothers were in eighth and ninth grade. When I left home, I didn't know how life would be for them with my mother. She had managed to blame my leaving home as the cause of her failed marriage. She fed that lie to my brothers, and they believed it.

I think that my youngest brother was in high school when he found out that my mother had not wanted him. We had just barely come to the United States when my mother got pregnant with him. She had wanted an abortion, but my father and step-grandfather tried to persuade her to keep the baby. My step-grandfather had convinced her by promising that he would take care of the baby. Looking back, that explains why my step-grandfather had always favored him. But for my brother, this revelation that our mother wanted to abort him affected him negatively. I can only guess that when she was angry at him for something, she blurted out, as she did with me, that she "should have aborted him."

Part of me felt remorse that I wasn't there to protect him; her anger was always turned toward me when I was there. I don't know how life was for them when I left home. But I know that he came to resent her. Somehow, I am grateful that my youngest brother wasn't scarred physically, as well as emotionally. I don't hear from him anymore and haven't seen him in years.

Her favorite was my middle brother—and, yes, children know who the parent's favorite child is. He could do no wrong in our mother's eyes. As a little girl, I was responsible for watching my brothers, and if anything happened to them or if they got into trouble, my mother would blame me for not keeping an eye on them.

When we were little, we played pretty rough with each other, but I always reminded them not to get hurt, or if they did, to not tell my mother. I told them not to do certain things because I would be the one punished for their actions. I don't think my brothers realized I took a lot of beatings for them. I tried not to resent them for it. I rationalized that it was not their fault and that they didn't know any better.

My brothers and I were close and would hang out together. We would walk for miles to Garden Grove in the summertime to visit our childhood friends and spend the whole day with them. I did my best to protect them. We grew apart during my teenage years and then after I left home.

My brothers are the only family that I have. But our mother managed to destroy that, as well. She ruined everything good. She had destroyed her marriage and managed to have her children hate and resent her, too. She favored my middle brother because he was always quiet, never challenged her, and let her vent without ever talking back to her.

By enduring years of abuse, I was the one who learned to rebel and challenge her.

ROAD TRIPS

I don't always want to remember my mother as bad or evil. I wish that I could have reached out to her toward the end of her life. Sometimes I think back and wish that I could have genuinely forgiven her and tried to start over again with her. Releasing the pain through this writing is my way of bringing forgiveness to all of us—for being traumatized humans, and certainly imperfect.

I remember spending time with our best childhood friends. We would take family trips together, and I wanted to be a part of their family. Their parents seemed to love and care for them and never yelled at them.

One year, we all went to Las Vegas and stayed at a cheap motel with a swimming pool so the kids could entertain themselves and go swimming. I was never a good swimmer. Somehow I got a cramp in my leg while I was swimming, and I went under. I couldn't get myself out of the water, and I was sinking. I held my breath as best as I could. My best friend's mother was there and saw that I wasn't coming up, so she jumped in and pulled me out of the water. If she wasn't there at that moment, I believe that I would have drowned. God looked out for me on that day, too.

Since that incident, even though I love to be near the water, being *in* the water causes me fear. I won't go in unless I can stand up, have something to hold onto, and can see the bottom.

We had so many favorite places that we would take road trips to in the summertime, and one of them was the Salton Sea, where we would go fishing. Road trips always meant going somewhere where we could either fish, go clamming, or pick fruit.

We took another road trip up to Redwood National Forest and Vancouver, Canada, camping all along the way. That was the most memorable trip for me. I loved driving through Oregon and Washington and seeing and smelling all those beautiful pine trees. I felt so small next to the grand mountains and towering pine trees. Living in Southern California, we didn't have those big trees, mountains, rivers, or lakes. I had never seen so much water, and I would never have guessed that forty years later, I would be calling the Pacific Northwest my home.

I know I am meant to be here with the mountains, trees, lakes, rivers, streams, and the ocean. I feel God here in this beautiful place of His making.

Our best childhood friends lived six miles away from us. As soon as our mother would leave for work, my brothers and I would walk over to their house, and we would hang out all day. We would play board games, walk across the street to the 7-Eleven, and play arcade games until we ran out of the quarters that their uncle had given us. The six of us would climb over a concrete fence to swim in their neighbor's pool while they were at work. We would make sure we got out of their yard before they got home. After dinner, my brothers and I would walk the six miles back home.

We would do this all summer for a couple of years, then one day, my mother told us we were not allowed to see them or talk to them anymore. I didn't know what happened, but I suspect that she did something to ruin that friendship. Those kids were like brothers and sisters; I had known them since I was five, and now she was taking away that friendship from me, too. Decades later, I found out why she ended that friendship; she confided to our best friends' mother that she wanted to leave her husband and kids. She was having an affair with a married man, and she wanted to leave us for him, but our friends' mother was a strong Christian and told my mother that what she was doing was wrong.

My mother, not tolerating anyone who disagreed with her, ended the friendship—ended *our* friendships—because my brothers and I were cut off, too.

Two Years

My mother was very traditional, and I was raised in a very traditional Cambodian culture. In our culture, we have prearranged marriages. I was sixteen when a family friend asked my mother if I could be one of her daughter's bridesmaid, and my mother gave her permission. She always chose my friends, and they were usually her friends' daughters. I struggled to relate to any of those girlfriends she chose for me. I saw their life as dull, heading toward regret and a life of unhappiness.

I wore traditional Cambodian wedding attire at the wedding, and it sounded like I had turned a few eyes. A few parents came to our house asking my parents for my hand in marriage to their son. Fear washed over me at the prospect of being married off at sixteen. Some of my girlfriends get married, got pregnant, and dropped out of school. I didn't want that life. I wanted to finish school, graduate from college, and have a career. I never wanted to be dependent on anyone. My experience so far had been miserable, and I wanted something else for my future.

My mother had picked a guy for me, and I was supposed to marry him. "Whatever you do," my father said, "try to get out of that marriage." He had raised me to be independent and wanted me to have an education and a career. He said that even though most everything in your life can be taken away at any time, nobody can take away your knowledge and skills. With knowledge and skills, you can make a new life anywhere, just like what he had done when we fled Cambodia to come to the United States. He did not want me ever to feel stuck in an unhappy marriage, dependent on a man to take care of me. He told me that if I had a great career, I would know that I could leave. I believe he knew what it felt like to be stuck in an abusive marriage, and he wanted to make sure that I would always have a way out.

I didn't know how I would get out of this predicament, but I knew that I needed to think of something fast. I told my mother that she couldn't marry me off because I was a minor, and she could get in trouble for marrying me off at that age. I don't even know if that was true. But, to my relief, she told me that I would be married as soon as I turned eighteen.

A couple of months later, the Cambodian community asked my parents for permission for me to be in a beauty pageant. My father said a firm, "No." He would *not* have men gawking at me. After my first time as a bridesmaid, I was asked me to be a bridesmaid in other people's weddings. But my father put a stop to that.

I had bought myself two years.

A daughter of my mother's friend had been married already and was under the control of her mother-in-law; if a mother-in-law didn't like a bride, they would make the young woman's life miserable or even try to break up the marriage.

One of my girlfriends was telling me about her wedding night. She had told me it was embarrassing. On their wedding night, there was a white sheet laid on the bed, and when they had consummated their marriage, it was expected to have some blood on it that would prove she was a virgin and untouched by any man. Both families would be waiting outside, and then the groom would let them into the room after the marriage was consummated. Both parents would look at the white sheet to make sure there was blood on it. If there was, all was well; if not, they would assume that she was not a virgin, thereby bringing shame onto herself and her family. The bride's family would have to repay the groom's family for the cost of the wedding and for the gift they had received from them.

Because the girl had brought shame to herself and her family, they would be shamed within the Cambodian community—where gossip spreads like wildfire—and their lives would be ruined.

When I heard this, I remembered my sexual abuse and suspected that at my wedding, there was a good chance I would disgrace my family.

I was always a runner. I ran cross country and was also in track and field. My mother always told me not to play sports so much because I could tear my hymen. I never understood what she meant until I heard my girlfriend telling me about her wedding night. I now understood why I was never allowed to wear a tampon because I could stretch or tear my hymen.

As soon as I turned eighteen, I made an appointment with a gynecologist to see if my hymen was still intact. He walked into the room with his female medical assistant, looked at me, and asked me if I was of marriage age. I nodded.

He examined me, told me that it was intact, and that is was okay to have sex—there is *nothing* shameful or dirty about it. I immediately thought, "*Maybe in your culture it is okay to have sex outside of marriage without any consequences, but not in my culture. You have no idea what my mother would do to me if I were not a virgin on my wedding night!"*

I pretended to agree with him, thanked him for his advice, and got out of there as fast as I could. It was embarrassing enough to let this man examine me, let alone listening to him talk about sex as something "natural."

The Foolish Plucketh

"Every wise woman buildeth her house:
but the foolish plucketh it down with her hands."

PROVERBS 14:1

Sometimes I was afraid that I would be like my mother and destroy my own family and everything that could be good in my life. Like my father, who was also abused as a child, I vowed to never be like my mother and never to hurt any children. I was concerned that I could be like her despite my intentions, so I was afraid to have children, although I desperately wanted them.

Looking back, I don't even know how I survived my past abuse. It had to be my faith and my will because no matter how hard she would beat me down, I refused to stay down. I had the will to live, to survive, and to make a better future for myself. I had hope, and without it, I would not be here. So many times, I sat in the dark by myself, pleading with God to take me home. I didn't want to suffer anymore, and

I didn't know how much longer I could take the physical, emotional, and mental abuse from my mother and the sexual abuse from my step-grandfather.

The very few that I shared my story with told me that I went through all that to help others overcome similar situations. But I didn't want to help others, and I didn't want to share my story. It was my past, and I wanted it buried.

I buried it so deep that I didn't even realize how bad it was affecting me. My relationships were shallow. Afraid of being rejected, I guarded my heart. A lifetime of abuse doesn't get fixed overnight. It takes decades to sort through all the emotions and pain. I had to truly learn to forgive and let go, but it was a process. I had to continually remind myself of all my positive traits.

Healing is an on-going process, as we are all works in progress. Once one thing is healed, the next layer of pain or trauma shows up to be seen and healed back into wholeness. I had to go through all those stages of grief: denial, anger, bargaining, depression, and acceptance. I was stuck in the anger phase for most of my twenties and in denial for almost most of my life. I have been bargaining with God since I was very young. Depression hit me in my late thirties through my forties.

Acceptance? Sometimes I doubt I will *ever* get to that stage.

AGE OF CONSENT

On my eighteenth birthday, of course, there was no birthday party. I had reached the age when my mother wanted to marry me off. I worked part-time after school to save up money for college and buy the essentials that I needed, such as clothes and school supplies. I gave the rest of the money to my mother to put away for college.

When I was sixteen, I worked at an auto store as a cashier and became friends with my boss, who was twelve years older than me. Most of his friends were Asian, so he knew a lot about Asian cultures. When I didn't have a car, he would give me a ride home because I worked until closing time, and he didn't want me to walk home in the dark. He and my mother had become friends, and I didn't think anything of it. My dad never liked him. To me, he was just a boss. We would talk at work, and he would give me a ride home when I didn't have a car or when my dad was unable to pick me up from work. He smoked like a chimney, and I hate the smell of cigarettes.

When I turned eighteen, he asked my parents for my hand in marriage. My father was against it, but my mother insisted that I marry him. He gave my mother $10,000 and bought me a new car and a massive engagement diamond ring—which I saw only once because my mother held onto it.

I knew there was no way I could get out of this prearranged marriage. I begged my mother to let me finish high school. She said that I was the only girl in the family, and I needed to do my duty and get married. She had gone to a lot of weddings to save up for this day. Many people owed her money from attending their family weddings, and she wanted to collect all that money back.

You see, in most Southeast Asian cultures, guests give money for the bride and groom. After the ceremony, the reception would most likely be at a Chinese restaurant that could hold fifty or more tables with ten chairs each. Each person at the wedding would give $50 or more. The bride and groom would go from table to table to collect envelopes with money in it. At the end of the reception, they would count the cash and use it to pay for all the food and tips. Anything that remained was given to the bride and groom to help them get a head start on their future together. Some of my friends had enough money for a down payment on their first home after all expenses were paid. But for me, that was not the case. My mother will be the one who keeping that money.

I told her that I did not want to get married, that I wanted to graduate from college first. She started crying and lamented how I would disgrace the family name if I didn't get married. I didn't see then how manipulative she could be, the way that she would cry until she got her way. I didn't want to marry someone who was twelve years older than me. I always envisioned myself marrying someone about my age so that we could build a future together. I wanted a loving family of my own. I didn't want to be anything like my mother or the family she raised and destroyed.

She told me to marry him and that after the wedding, I could always leave him. A traditional Cambodian wedding did not require a legal marriage certificate. People would get married the traditional way and be considered a married couple. If they wanted to get married in a church and make it legal, they could do that, too. I was stupid enough to believe her again, and I agreed to marry him. To make sure that I didn't back out of the traditional wedding or leave him, he and my mother took me to Las Vegas to have an official wedding. Once I was legally married to him, I wouldn't be able to leave.

After we officially got married, I refused to let him touch me. My mother had planned a big traditional wedding and, of course, the reception dinner so she could collect her money. I could not imagine being married to this man for life. I wanted out and didn't know how to get out of it. I told him that if he wanted a virgin for a wife, I was not the one for him and that I was not a virgin. But he said that it didn't matter to him if I was a virgin or not. He wanted me, had loved me since I was sixteen, and had been waiting patiently for me to turn eighteen so that he could marry me. He knew that the only person he had to convince was my mother. That was why he and my mother were close. My father probably knew it, which was why he didn't like him.

Of course, I was kept in the dark. I felt betrayed by my parents and hated my mother even more for doing this to me.

She had planned a huge traditional wedding. I had one girlfriend whom I trusted. She was also a Christian, and we would go to church together on Sundays. I called her and told her what was going on. She had no clue of anything I was going through. She asked me about my boyfriend—had I told him any of this? No, I hadn't told anyone. She insisted that I tell him and that he had a right to know what was going on.

I decided to tell him. He told me to get out of that marriage and live with him and his mother. I was so tormented I didn't know what to do. I did not love this man, and I did not want to spend the rest of my life with him. I told my mother that I wanted a divorce and that I would not get married the traditional way. She yelled and screamed at me, asking me why, if I didn't want to marry him, why did I marry him in the first place?

I walked away, thinking, *"How will I get out of this mess?*

All I ever wanted was a normal childhood, to be a normal teenager, and have a normal life. But there was one obstacle after another. Finally, I told my husband that my mother had made me marry him and that I wanted a divorce. He responded that he would never allow me to divorce him and that if I did file for it, he would contest it.

I was trapped.

A BETTER LIFE

I had been working and saving money since I was twelve. My first job was working at a donut shop on the weekends from 5 a.m. until 6 p.m. for $40 a weekend. Then, as soon as I turned sixteen, I got a worker's permit and worked for minimum wage, which was a step up. I would go to work after school and until closing at 10 p.m. Until I got my car, I would walk home in the dark, praying that nothing bad would happen to me. God was always there protecting me.

When I was seventeen, my mother was furious one day, and I didn't know why. I walked away from her, which seemed to enrage her even more. She went to the garage, and then I saw her walking back into the house with an ax.

"Oh, dear God, that woman has lost it and is going to chop me to pieces."

As she ran after me with that ax, I ran into my bedroom and locked the door right as she swung the ax at the door. I ran to the bedroom window and jumped outside, where I ran to a convenience store nearby to call my boyfriend to pick me up. He didn't think I should go back home, so I stayed at his house with his mother for a couple of days.

My boyfriend and I met at work during my sophomore year of high school. We were cashiers. He had approached me one day after work and asked if I wanted to hang out with him. I told him that my mother would not allow it. But we always chatted and hung out at work. I didn't have anyone I was close with, and he was the first person I truly felt connected to. Eventually, we started spending time together outside of work. I would tell my parents that I was going to work when I was really going to be with him.

He brought me over to his house one day to meet his mother, and she told me that she had heard so much about me from him. Ever since that first meeting, she was like a mother to me and offered me loving advice. She showed me what a mother's love was and never yelled at him or belittled him. She only spoke loving words of encouragement to her son.

After he introduced me to his friends while they were drinking alcohol and smoking weed, I knew he would never be "the one." Later, I found out that he was also doing ecstasy, but just not around me because he knew that I didn't use drugs.

I had stayed away from doing drugs because my life was already a mess without making it worse! I didn't have a loving mother like his, who would always be there for me. If I were a drug addict or an alcoholic, my mother would most likely have beaten me senseless!

I couldn't understand how he could be such a mess with a mother like that. If she were my mother, I would have gone far in life. It was because of her that I wasn't ready to let him go.

Eventually, she told me that I should leave her son because I was too good for him. I was so determined to make a better life for myself and not let a man get in the way of achieving my goals and dreams.

I stayed with him longer than I should have because I felt sorry for him and thought I could help him. Now when I look back at my life, I see how I was always trying to help someone or fix someone. Perhaps because I couldn't help or fix myself...

A few days after my mother tried to chop down my door, I went back home. She asked me where I had stayed those past few days. "With a friend," I said.

We dated for two years, and I hid it well from my parents. Then one day, my mother found out that I was dating him. She had my Dad drive her to my work, where she saw that my car wasn't there. She became furious with me for lying to her, but I couldn't tell her I was dating someone. I just wanted to be a typical teenager who had friends and went on dates for once in my life. I was just holding hands and hugging, nothing more. For God's sake, I was not even capable of loving! I had never loved or trusted anyone.

When I got home, my mother confronted me, and I told her that I was dating someone. She accused me of being a whore and said that I was like a dog who would do any guy in the car, that I would amount to nothing, and that I was a loser! Her words cut like a knife and hurt to the core because God is more important to me than anyone—especially any guy. Even though I had been tainted and defiled as a child against my own will, I still believed in saving myself for marriage.

She took the car away from me. I was so angry at her, I called my boyfriend to come get me, and I just walked out. I was done. I was angry about her accusations. My thoughts were going everywhere, and in my anger I thought, "*Since*

I am already accused of doing something that I haven't even done with him, I might as well just do it."

I can't believe that I allowed her to let me sink so low. That night we had sex, and the next morning, I got up, took a shower, and cried all day. I cried for a week. I had done something that was so against my belief system, and I regretted it. Had I sunk so low? I hated myself for letting her get the best of me. Shame permeated me.

⁂

For years, I had been cashing my checks and giving my mother all the money to save for college.

When I graduated from high school, I asked for my money. She told me that she didn't have it and had spent it all. I had no way to pay for college now. I didn't qualify for financial aid because my Dad made too much money, even though we were just getting by. I didn't know what else to do, so I decided to work full-time and go to school part-time.

I tried doing this for a semester but realized that I wouldn't get very far that way. Something had to change.

OUTCAST

I refused to live with my husband or let him touch me. But I could never file for divorce because I couldn't afford attorney fees. I was still in high school, and I needed to finish—graduating from high school was my priority.

At this point, I didn't care if I brought shame to the family or myself, so I told my mother that I would not stay married to him and that I would not show up if she had a traditional wedding.

I no longer cared about people spreading rumors about me. I needed to live for myself instead of for my mother. She told me if I did not want to stay married to him, to get out of the house. So that's what I did. I called my boyfriend and told him that I was given the option to stay married or get out of the house. He drove over and waited outside for me as I packed all my clothes. I took a couple of bags full of clothes and left.

I was scared. I didn't know what the future would hold for me. Despite it all, I managed to get good grades and graduated from high school. But after high school, I would have to figure out how I was going to live. College had always been in my future, and I knew I had to go—whatever it took—because that was the only way that I would be able to make a future for myself and escape this life of poverty.

With all of the money I had given my mother to save for college gone, and her refusal to give me a penny, I knew I would get nowhere fast if I worked full-time and went to school part-time.

So I joined the military. I simply left and didn't tell my family or my husband. It was *my* life, and I was going to make a life for myself. I was done living for everyone else.

I have walked down a dark road alone for so many decades with a wall built up around me. I never let anyone get too close, and I didn't want them to know my past because I did not want their sympathy. I didn't want to be judged or seen as the bad, defiant daughter who didn't respect her mother. When given a choice to stay married or get out of the house, I left. I was the "slut" who joined the military in the hopes of building a better future for herself. I was the one who left my husband for a lover and then left him, too, for the military. I was the one nobody wanted their daughter to associate with. I had heard it all from my mother and her friends. I was an outcast within my own family and among my community. I had no one.

I was stuck between two cultures and never felt that I belonged to either. I believed in traditional Cambodian cultural values, but I was also westernized, and I wanted to make my own decisions. I didn't want to be dependent on a man to take care of me, and I never wanted to feel trapped, controlled, or abused by anyone ever again.

I believe that my will to survive and desire to have a better future for myself, while never losing hope or faith was what got me through those many dark days.

BE ALL YOU CAN BE

In November 1990, I joined the Army. I spoke with a United States Army recruiter who said that once I completed my duty term, I would qualify for the Army College Fund and the GI Bill. I enlisted for two years, plus Basic Training, Advanced Individual Training (AIT), and four years of Army Reserves.

I had to leave to try to make a better life for myself, free from my mother's control and abuse. I had always been a stubborn person, refusing to cry when she would beat me and refusing to let her see that she had gotten the best of me. My stubbornness, my will to survive, and my drive to succeed had gotten me this far, and I didn't know how far I could go.

I went for the shortest service term because my goal was to go to college and graduate as fast as possible. I intended to go back in as an officer once I graduated from college.

I enlisted without telling my family or my husband that I was leaving to go to Basic Training. In November 1990, I flew out of the San Diego Airport and headed to Fort Dix in New Jersey. I remember stepping out of the bus in Fort Dix with the drill sergeants yelling at us and thinking to myself, *"Oh, God, what have I gotten myself into?* But I was determined to get through it. I was accustomed to being yelled at and told what to do, so I did as I was told without complaint. I kept to myself. My mother had always chosen my friends, and I noticed that the girls in Basic Training were different. I had to grow up fast.

When I left to join the Army, I intended to leave everything painful behind and start a new life. I was going to let my mother go. When I came back home that Christmas break, I told my boyfriend that if he couldn't quit drinking and doing drugs, it was best that we go our separate ways. I set out on this journey alone. I had always been alone.

Decades later, I reconnected with my first boyfriend, thanks to Facebook. Just as I had predicted, he was an alcoholic and had a few DUIs on his record. I tried to help him, but he didn't see himself as an alcoholic, and I decided I didn't want any toxic people in my life.

Snow Globe

I woke one morning and looked outside to see the streets and trees covered with snow. For some reason, the sight of the snow and watching the snow fall brought joy and happiness to my heart. I have always loved the snow. Standing at my window and watching the sun trying to come out of the cloud and catching a glimpse of its rays was just an amazing sight. The tree branches were iced over with icicles and glistened in the sun. An ordinary street had turned into a winter wonderland overnight. I was reminded that morning how beautiful and majestic God is, and I couldn't wait to see heaven.

Growing up in Orange County, California, I didn't get to see any snow. I don't ever remember going to the mountains when there was snow on it. My first fond memory of snow was while stationed in Hanau, Germany. My roommate woke me up at 5 a.m. and told me to look outside. Everything was covered with snow. I ran out with only my pajamas on. I laid on the snow and looked up at the sky—it was so clear and blue. I made snow angels and attempted to build a snowman.

When it was time to line up for our morning workout, my squad leader and platoon sergeant could not get me to line up—I was so excited about playing in the snow. I think they had no idea how to handle me. There were only two women in our company—me and my roommate. So, they let me play in the snow all day.

After that, I was sick in bed for a week. When I woke up, my roommate and my boyfriend were sitting by my bed playing cards. I couldn't remember anything. I asked what happened, and they told me I was knocked out for a couple of days; they thought I had pneumonia. They were worried about me, so one of them was always with me to make sure I was doing okay.

That incident didn't change how I felt about snow, just what I wore to play in it. I would go to the mountains and drive in it for hours. It is magical to me. Something about breathing the cold crisp air and seeing the ground and trees covered with snow brought warmth to my heart. I am so grateful for that joy.

Making a Break for It

It was Christmas break, and we had the option to take leave and go home or stay on base. I chose to stay on base—and I was the only one. My drill sergeant asked me why I wasn't going home. I told him that no one back home knew that I was leaving to join the military and that I had been running away from a prearranged marriage and didn't want to see the man I'd married or the mother who had made me marry him.

Somehow, my drill sergeant encouraged me to go home and make amends with my mother. He told me it was not too late to get a flight back home. I called my mother and told her where I was, and she started crying, saying she was worried about me because she had not heard from me in months. She begged me to come home for the holidays. I agreed, thinking that maybe she had changed.

She had not. She accused me of being a slut; by her logic, only bad girls join the military. She said that I was good for nothing and would never amount to anything. Her girlfriends wouldn't let their daughters associate with me. Worst of all, my mother called my husband. He went to my recruiter's office and caused a scene, saying that they had no right to enlist his wife. They hadn't asked if I was married, and I hadn't volunteered the information. I had never changed my last name because I planned to get an annulment as soon as I could afford it.

The only person who was proud of me was my father. He told all his friends that his daughter had joined the Army, how proud he was of me, and that I was falling in his footsteps. He told me it doesn't matter what other people think of me; all that matters is that I know the truth. People will judge no matter what I do, good or bad, he told me, so brush it off, don't let it affect you. My whole life has been spent proving my mother wrong and that I was not, as she always said, a worthless dog.

My secret revenge on my mother and her friends who called me bad and worthless was to become successful at whatever I did and make them eat their words. I imagined that their daughters were the ones who would not amount to much while I succeeded. I did succeed in the end, but with a price:

Loneliness.

In the Army Now

Basic training was hard, but then—my life had always been challenging. I had learned to survive, but going through basic training made me stronger mentally.

After basic training, I did AIT at Fort Leonard Wood, Missouri. My military occupational specialty (MOS) was 62E—a light equipment operator. After completing my AIT, I was bound to head overseas. In fact, I had *asked* to be stationed overseas. I wanted to be as far away from my family and my past life as I possibly could be. I was stationed in Hanau, Germany, shortly before the base closed.

I was young, naive, and gullible. However, in the military, I was no saint. I could finally live as I wanted!

A week before my duty station was determined, I wandered the streets of Frankfort one evening and meandered into a bar. There were two men at the bar, and I sat alone at the bar in my uniform away from them.

One of them kept asking me if I wanted to go upstairs. I glanced upstairs, thinking that maybe there was another bar there, but I didn't see anything.

"No," I told him. *Why does he keep asking me to go upstairs?*

I saw a woman walk downstairs with one man, then go back upstairs with another one. Then it dawned on me... I am in a place where prostitution is legal.

I already thought so little of men, and this added to my disdain. I was out of there as fast as possible!

When I got to my duty station, I told my roommate about the incident. She laughed and told me I was most likely in the red-light district, and to stay away from there! As if I was going to go *there* again! After that experience, I knew life was going to get interesting for me in Germany.

No matter how much shame my mother tried to heap on me, I didn't regret my decision to join the military. For a few years, I escaped her grasp. I had been surviving on my own ever since I could remember, but now I finally saw that no one had been looking out for me but me. I chose not to play the poor-me victim game. I refused to be beaten down, let alone stay down. Everyone has a choice, and I chose my own path. Even so, it wasn't easy learning to live a healthy and functional life when I didn't know what that life looked like.

In the Army, I learned that I was not good at relationships. I had a bad history with men, especially my abusive step-grandfather, my manipulative husband, and my addicted ex-boyfriend. Also, I usually had another man waiting in the wings if my current boyfriend didn't work out.

It was always easy for me to sever ties because I didn't trust anyone, and if I see a relationship going nowhere, I let it go. But now, I was looking for that special person, someone I could connect with and feel safe and protected by.

Am I incapable of true love?

I was looking for an equal partner, to share goals, interests, and values with. I always knew that the man I would marry would be a Christian. In every relationship, it felt like something was missing. I would go looking for that something to fill that void—but nothing did.

My first boyfriend in the military was sweet, kind, and gentle, the son of a preacher. I don't know why I ended things with him after two months. He had never been with any woman before me, and I was his first love. He truly loved me, and I broke his heart.

Shortly after I got to my duty station in Germany, one weekend, the guys in my company were going on a trip and invited me along. Of course, I wanted to see Germany! We went for a drive, and they pulled this thing that looked like beef jerky. They handed it to me and asked me if I wanted some. I said no because I didn't feel like eating any beef jerky. Then they started smoking it. Thank goodness I didn't eat it! Later I realized it was hashish. One of my boyfriends in the military smoked it.

My next relationship lasted nine months. This guy was as stubborn and hardheaded as I was, and we fought a lot. He was a pretty boy with blonde hair and blue eyes. We were in an engineering company and would repair military roads. I was in Mannheim, and he was in Wildflecken for a few months. One weekend I decided to surprise him and took the train up to Wildflecken. There, he told me he was sleeping with a married woman. This was during Desert Storm, and her husband was in the Gulf War. I felt sick to my stomach, realizing that I had opened myself up to a man who would stoop so low as to sleep with a woman with two children whose husband was in a war zone risking his life.

He had broken the soldiers' code. He tried to tell me that he didn't love her and it was only sex and that she knew that he had a girlfriend. My heart was broken. I was a total mess, so much so that I couldn't take the train back. I took a taxi ride—a costly taxi ride from Wildflecken to Mannheim. This was when I started having a back-up guy, usually a close friend who I could hang out with and vent because I couldn't trust a boyfriend. After he cheated on me with a married woman, this man married my lesbian roommate (which, of course, didn't last long).

I never trusted any man after that.

I moved on quickly, dating his best friend, who was six feet four inches tall. Other than height, we had a lot in common, both focusing on our career goals. But I got tired of everyone making fun of our height difference, so I broke it off with him. I'm sorry that I ever hurt him, and I wish I were at a better place at that time.

I dated a man who everyone called my "Ken doll." He was from Alabama and had a son with his high school girlfriend. I was *not* about to get serious with someone who already had a child! Our relationship was tumultuous. We were both hard-headed, strong-willed, and stubborn. I stayed with him for nine months, just until I got out of the military.

I learned a lot about myself during these years, including that I wasn't ready to be in a committed relationship. Because I was finally free from the grasp of my mother and the watchful eye of my step-grandfather, I was reluctant to be under anyone's control. I was becoming like my mother: pushing everyone away.

I even pushed God away, growing apart from Him when I left for the Army. Until then, I had lived under the control of my mother. I tried my best to be independent, to think for myself, and to discover who I was as a person, but it was difficult while under her control. No matter how hard I tried to resist her choices for me, I still wound up doing what she wanted me to do.

Leaving for the military gave me a freedom that I never had. I experienced a wider world, like a small fish swimming in the vast ocean alone. Up until then, I was able to keep my focus on creating a better life. But now, I wasn't sure how to navigate out of harm's way and avoid corruption, so I stayed away from anything that would hinder or hurt me.

No matter how terrible my past was, I now had a choice. I could let it eat at me, destroy me, or even consume me—or, I could own my power and refuse. To protect myself, I refused to look back, even when I had flashbacks.

However, my choice brought so much anger to the surface that I had to deal with before I could ever found peace.

I knew I had to file for divorce before I got back to the United States. My husband would contest the divorce if I filed State-side, but he was unlikely to travel to Germany. So, while I was in Germany, I saved up enough money and filed for an annulment. The divorce was finalized a couple of months before I headed back to the States.

When my service contract ended in March 1992, I was honorably discharged. One of my friends from the Army was retiring. He and his wife were like parents to me and invited me to live with them in Texas. He was interested in becoming a long-distance truck driver and thought maybe we could do that together. I told him that I wanted to go to college. I wasn't sure where I was going to live, but I was not going home. I thought maybe I could settle in South

Carolina. I could do my Reserves at the base there, get a small apartment, find a part-time job, and enroll in school full-time.

I called my mother to tell her that I was getting out of the Army and was thinking about living in South Carolina. She cried and begged me to come back home. She said that in the two and a half years that I had been gone, she had missed me and had changed, which was my deepest desire.

Perhaps God had saved her as He had saved me.

Believing her—again—was my mistake.

CIVILIAN LIFE

It was difficult to readjust to civilian life—and living with my mother again. I had to buy a car and decided to buy a used one with cash, which took a chunk out of my savings. My mother charged me rent, which was another expense. When I was in the military, I had put money in a CD so that I wouldn't touch it until it was time to pay for college. But then I needed to pay for tuition a few months before the terms of my CD ended. I asked my mother if I could borrow $500 from her and pay her back in a couple of months. She told me that she didn't have the money. What was I thinking, asking her for help? She had never helped me with anything. My retired friend and his wife loaned me the money, and I repaid them within a few months without paying any penalties.

My mother and I argued all the time. I'd go dancing with a friend on weekends, and my mother thought my friend was corrupting me and hated her for it. She even slashed the roof of her convertible car with a knife. We both knew it was my mother, though we had no proof. I wouldn't tolerate her verbal or emotional abuse anymore, which only angered her more. I told her that because I was paying rent, I would come and go as I pleased.

On my second day back home, I went to get an eye exam at Sears because I needed contact lenses. When I wandered out into the mall, a man approached me, started a conversation, and asked if I wanted to go to the movies with him. Why not? I did panic a bit after I got into his truck and realized that I was in a vehicle with a stranger... but I figured if he tried anything, I could always kick him and jump out of the car. But there was no need. We became friends, and we would hang out at my place or go out somewhere.

My mother liked him a lot and thought I should marry him because he was a good man. I thought, "*Here we go again with this marriage thing.*" I was nowhere ready to get married. I just want to try to figure out my place in this world. She told me that she saw him in her dream and that he was the man meant for me. She bought two wedding rings and told me to give one to him and that we needed to get married. At that time, I didn't realize that my mother was paranoid that my best girlfriend would try to chase after him; that was why she insisted that I married him. I didn't love him, and I knew that would be a big mistake on my part.

I was right. I wasn't capable of having feelings for people, especially not love. I had never loved anyone. How could I marry someone I didn't love? But she kept on nagging and insisting that I marry him. Being the submissive daughter, I obeyed. One morning, I showed up at his door with two wedding bands and told him that my mother had bought them and said we should get married.

Six months later, we went to Las Vegas with my mother and got married. This was my second wedding in Las Vegas with my mother. After we got married, she wanted to plan a big Cambodian ceremony and reception because she had many people who owed her money from all the weddings that she had attended. Had she talked me into marrying so she could make money off me? I refused to have a Cambodian wedding. I didn't want to see her friends, and I didn't want to hear any more gossip about me.

After I got married, my father asked me to promise him that I would go to school, finish school, and leave whenever I wanted to. I promised. I would not stay stuck.

Married Life

The first three or four years of our marriage were rough. I had become angry and hateful. We lived with my mother for a couple of years, and it felt like our marriage was doomed to fail as long as we were living with her. She hated my girlfriend and didn't want her coming around the house, afraid she would try to steal my husband. When my husband and I fought, my mother would defend him. In her eyes, he could do no wrong. With her meddling in our business, we were never able to resolve or work anything out on our own. But I was determined to make our marriage work. After all, I had gotten him into this mess.

After a couple of years, she wanted to raise our rent. We knew that we could get our own place for the amount she wanted, so we did. Then she offered to keep the rent the same, but my husband told her no, we already found an apartment.

Our marriage was much less rocky without her interference.

Around the time we moved into our own apartment, I felt God calling me back. He had put it in my heart to read my Bible, pray, and start looking for a church. My husband encouraged me to find a church home for us, and I did.

God had put it in my heart to call one of my childhood friends who used to go to the same church as I did before I left for the military. I told her that God had wanted me to talk to her about something, but I didn't know what! We met for lunch, and she shared the Gospel with me in a way that she hadn't been able to do when we were kids. I accepted it in a way that I hadn't been able to as a scared kid. I knew that I needed God. I knew that I was angry and needed the unconditional love of God. He had always been there for me. Even though I had walked away from Him, He still loves, forgives, and calls me back home.

My husband was an electrician and started his own business.

I graduated from nursing school in December 1997 and became a nurse. We bought our own home. I finally had the normal life that I had always wanted. Or so I thought.

The first few years of our marriage were difficult. We lived with my mother, and when we argued, she would take his side. I resented him for that. Once we moved out of her house and into a place of our own, we could better resolve our issues. But things were not perfect. I'm a city girl, and his grandparents raised my husband in a small town in Kentucky, so he wanted to move somewhere rural.

I'm practical, and love is abstract. In my mid to late twenties, I became a born-again Christian. God was working on me to transform my cold heart into a loving one. I prayed for my husband, and my pastor invited him to dinner and Bible study and shared the Gospel with him. My husband was saved.

From the outside, it looked like I had it all: a career, a home, and a loving husband.

God had helped me let go of the hate and anger from my past.

But now, it seemed like my husband was absorbing all the negativity that I had released. I had hidden a lot from him. He knew that my mother had abused me when I was a child, but I had never shared details. I also never told him that I had been sexually abused. That secret was dirty, shameful, and carefully hidden. I would bear that pain alone.

Even though I knew that childhood abuse victims were statistically more likely to become abusers, I fantasized that my past would be forgotten if I had my own children. There would be no chance of me hurting them as I had been hurt.

But, my higher self wasn't convinced. I was afraid to have children.

Nothing Like My Mother

My girlfriend asked me if I would be her baby's godmother, and I gladly agreed. I have always loved children and wanted to have children of my own if I hadn't been so afraid. I was split: part of me wanted to have the happy family I never had; part of me was afraid I would have a family like the one I grew up with.

My godson was my pride and joy. God had brought him into my life for a reason—to teach me patience and love. He was a handful, and he triggered me many times. And throughout it all, I never had a desire ever to hurt him or lay a hand on him.

He showed me that I could be a loving mother—that I am capable of loving.

While my friend was going to school, I would care for her son on my days off. I cared for him from infancy until he was eight or nine. When he was a toddler, he had a thing about being naked. I would leave the room he would take off his clothes and his diaper and run around naked. I would frequently have to put his diapers and clothes back on. When I left the room, he would take it all off again. I thought, *"What is his mother going to think of him running around with no clothes or diapers on?"* Finally, I just gave up, and when his mother picked him up, I told her about it and said I didn't know what to do. Apparently, he was doing the same thing at home.

He would break things, then lie about it and blame his younger brother. At times when he left my house, I would find broken stuff underneath the area rug. He wouldn't listen and would flat out refuse to do what I asked. One day when he was about seven, he pushed me hard. I cried because I didn't know how to handle him. I told him that I didn't know how to handle him and that I didn't know what to do about his behavior. He promised me that he would be good—which lasted about an hour.

When he was four, I put him in "time out" in my rocking chair and told him that he was to sit there and not get up. He peed on my rocking chair. When I asked him why, he responded that I told him he was supposed to sit there and not get up.

When he was eight, I took him and his younger brother to a pumpkin patch. I told them to make sure they used the restroom before leaving because it is a long ride back home. He insisted that he didn't have to go, but he had to pee about twenty minutes later. We were stuck in traffic on an overhead bridge, and there was nowhere for me to get off the freeway. He told me to pull over, but I couldn't. So, naturally, he peed on himself in my car. Surprisingly, I wasn't triggered or upset in the least.

I was allowing love in.

It was through this boy that God showed me that I am nothing like my mother. At the age of thirty-three, I was finally ready to have children and start my family, knowing that I would be a kind and loving mother.

Wanting Children

We tried having children for about a year with no luck. We went and saw a fertility specialist through our insurance. I had some testing done and was told that I couldn't have children. I was devastated when I heard that I was infertile, and I cried because I knew the reason deep inside. I had never been on any birth control pills and had never gotten pregnant.

The past sexual abuse that I had suppressed for so long had come back to haunt me.

Our insurance did not cover in-vitro fertilization, but we saw a fertility specialist and went that route anyway. I had to inject hormones subcutaneously daily to release multiple eggs. Then I had to have another injection in the deep muscles of my buttocks. My buttocks were red and swollen. At times I couldn't sit. I would get hot flashes and was overly emotional. I would cry just watching a commercial.

But the embryo implant was a success, and I had gotten pregnant. I was elated. I was going to have my own family. I could correct all the wrongs that had been done to me. I would be the mother that my mother was never to me. At six weeks gestation, we heard our baby's heartbeat at an ultrasound.

That joy didn't last long.

I was about eight weeks pregnant when I had some spotting, then suddenly I started to have abdominal cramping, and my stomach hurt terribly. I knew in my heart I was having a miscarriage, but I was in denial and pleaded with God to please save my baby. I told my husband that he had to take me to the emergency room. They took me in and did an ultrasound on me. I didn't hear any heartbeat and could see from her face that something wasn't right. They got the obstetrician, who informed us that I had a miscarriage, and the baby's heart was no longer beating.

I cried.

She wanted to do a dilation and curettage, but I wouldn't let her. I told her that I wanted my fertility specialist to confirm this before deciding on the procedure. I made an appointment to see my fertility specialist, who confirmed that I had a miscarriage. I was hurt and angry.

"God, why did you take my baby away from me?"

My fertility specialist suggested that we try a second time. I had to endure going through all those injections again. And this time, it was worse. I was bruised and developed lumps everywhere. It was getting hard to find a place without any hematomas to inject in my buttocks. The second in-vitro fertilization implant was not successful.

Our fertility specialist recommended a third trial, but I couldn't emotionally go through the pain and heartache of another failed procedure. We opted out.

My godson's mother and my sister-in-law wanted to help and told us that they wanted to be a surrogate mother, but my husband refused. If anything happened to them while having a baby for us, he wouldn't be able to forgive himself. So, we had to look at other options for having children.

Secret Revealed

Sex with my husband was triggering memories and flashbacks of my childhood sexual trauma. I knew that I had to tell him about my past sexual abuse and why I couldn't have children.

I withdrew. I didn't want to be touched by any man. The sight of men disgusted me. I knew I had to overcome that somehow. I struggled with it. I didn't want anyone to know what I was going through, and I was going through all of this alone, but my two best friends knew me too well. They knew I was going through something painful. They kept asking me what was wrong, so I finally told them. They reminded me that I was only a little girl and that I did nothing wrong.

I don't give up easily. I pushed through it again by pushing it aside, staying in denial and not dealing with my pain. I was so good at pretending that there was nothing wrong and ignoring my feelings.

My husband and I talked about adoption and applied with an agency. A social worker came to our house and interviewed us. She asked why we wanted children, and we both told her that I couldn't have children and that we had tried in vitro fertilization. We didn't bring up my past childhood abuse because we thought it was irrelevant.

She told me that I needed to see a psychologist and gave me a list of psychologists in our city. I made an appointment to see one. She informed me that I needed a letter from a psychologist stating that I was emotionally and mentally healthy and that I would not be negatively affected by the adoption process. I needed "a mental bill of health" from the psychologist.

It was a big mistake.

On the first visit, we talked about my infertility and how I felt about it. The second visit went a little deeper, including why I was infertile and what had happened to me, which opened up a whole can of worms.

She asked me to come back the following week to continue where we had left off. But, having opened up to her about my childhood sexual abuse, I was feeling extreme and negative emotions surfacing. She wasn't helping me deal with the anxiety, depression, and anger my memories had brought back up.

Then she wanted me to write a letter to my step-grandfather, even though he was dead. How was that supposed to help me? What answer could he possibly give me from his grave for what he did to me? My depression worsened, and I started having suicidal thoughts.

Then we talked about my mother, and the psychiatrist wanted to make an appointment with both of us. That wasn't going to happen. I knew my mother too well; she had already denied ever abusing me when I had asked her for an explanation for why she treated me the way she did.

My best friend saw my depression and isolation. I had always been sociable and hung out with friends, but now I kept them at a distance. I didn't want to be near anyone. I just wanted to be alone. She was persistent and kept asking me what was wrong, so I told her about my psychologist and how, after every visit, I would leave feeling worse. She suggested that I stop going. So, I stopped going and instead made an appointment with my primary care provider to get on an anti-depressant.

My friend recommended a Christian psychologist. During the first visit, I sat for an hour and didn't say a word. I wasn't sure if I was ready to go through that deep excavation again. On the second visit, I opened up a little to see what her response would be. I liked her approach because she would quote scriptures and would send me home with verses to read to help me get through whatever problem we were talking about during my session.

Somehow, I developed a dependency on her and couldn't think or make decisions for myself without asking her first. So I stopped going. Without going through a psychologist, a U.S. adoption was out for us. We began looking at overseas adoption.

My husband didn't want a child who wasn't Cambodian or Caucasian, because he didn't think it was fair for that child to have parents that were not of the same race. I didn't see it that way. To me, a child is a child, and every child, whether from a different race or not, deserves a loving home and a chance of a better life. We tried to adopt from Cambodia, but the United States had closed adoption to Cambodia because of child-trafficking. All I wanted was to have children and start a new life with my own family. I wanted what I never had as a child, and I still believed that having my own family would make my childhood trauma fade away.

I was still living in denial.

Yes, and Amen

My father was the one person in my life who was stable. However, his life had been challenging, as well. He was abused by his father and ran away when he was little to seek shelter at the Buddhist temple. Then he married my mother, who never loved him and who had also abused him. Our lives are not too different from each other. At times I've wondered if I would still be here if he hadn't tried to protect me from the worst of my mother's abuse. Would she have wanted to kill me?

When he divorced my mother, he married a younger wife. She was thirteen years older than me. None of his children liked her. She was nice—until she started drinking, and then she was mean. She had a son and a daughter. My brothers and I accepted her children as our brother and sister, and we tried to look out for them. But she was like my mother in that she destroyed everything. She kept her children away from us. My brothers were still living at home when our father remarried, and their new stepmother destroyed that relationship, too. She would get drunk and pick a fight with my brothers and made my Dad choose between her or them. She put him in a difficult position, and he chose her. She was his wife. My brothers were hurt, and my mother fed them lies about my Dad to fuel the fire. Both of my brothers did not want to have anything to do with my Dad.

One of my brothers refused to have anything to do with him ever again, and never let our father meet his wife and children. He and his wife live in Las Vegas, and they drove down to Orange County almost every month for years. They would always stay with my mother. My sister-in-law and I would plead with my brother to let my father meet his grandson. My brother wouldn't allow it. One weekend, when the boy was a toddler, my sister-in-law and I took him to meet his grandfather, anyway.

I wish I had spent more time with my father, but I didn't because I couldn't stand my stepmother. She was a mean drunk. When she started drinking, she would cause an argument for no reason. I stayed away from them and mostly visited my father when his new wife was at work. I didn't see him much—and then in December 2007, God put it in my heart to reach out to him. I hadn't seen him since earlier that year, and when I went to his house, he looked frail and weak. He was dying from cancer and hadn't told any of his children because he didn't want to bother us. I called my brothers for them to come and visit him. My middle brother refused.

Within a month, our father was hospitalized. I had decided to bring him home on hospice care. But that day, when he was supposed to be discharged to hospice, God put an urgency in my heart to give him the Gospel. The difficulty was that I didn't speak Cambodian that well. I called my pastor—my dearest friend since I was a teenager—and told him that my father was in the hospital and was dying. He came right away. I felt called to make his funeral arrangements. As I was leaving the hospital, my pastor arrived, so I updated him about my Dad. He went to give my Dad the Gospel while I went to make the arrangements.

When I was with Dad before I left to make the funeral arrangements, he was alert and coherent, but he took a turn for the worse as soon as I left. While I was gone, he developed a blood clot to his leg, which caused a pulmonary embolism. By the time my pastor came upstairs, my father was barely holding on. But he listened, and his last words were "yes" and "amen." He had accepted the Gospel, and I will see him again someday in heaven.

My brother and his girlfriend—now his wife—were there when our father passed. But I didn't get a chance to say goodbye to him. We all sat there by his side until they took his body away.

I called my other brother and my sister-in-law and told them that he passed away. I didn't want to tell my mother and hear her say something terrible about him. But my brothers thought that she had a right to know. So, I went over to my mother's house to tell her. She said to me in Cambodian that he deserved to die and that she was glad that he was not around anymore. I got upset and just left. My stepdad, who is Caucasian and doesn't understand the Cambodian language, wondered why I was so upset. I can only imagine his wife made something up.

After that, I wanted nothing to do with my mother and stayed away from her as much as I possibly could. I couldn't understand how she could have so much hatred in her heart for him. She had verbally and physically abused him—and made him out to be the one at fault. When I was younger, I had wished that she would die. But over time, God had slowly softened my heart, and I couldn't imagine wishing my worst enemy dead.

With my father's death, I had many regrets. I wished that I had spent more time with him and didn't allow my stepmother to keep me away. After he had passed away, my stepmother told me that while he was sick and knew that he was dying, he would say to her that his daughter would come to see him. Luckily, by the grace of God, I *did* go see him before he passed.

I wish that he could have lived a happier life, but I know he is now in a better place. I can't wait to see him in heaven—my God is amazing. I had prayed for a decade for my father's salvation, and God had answered my prayer with so little time left.

Never Again

One day, I was sick. My husband, who didn't want me to be home alone, dropped me off at my mother's house while he was at work. I didn't want to go because I didn't trust my mother, and I was feeling weak. I knew I couldn't handle her that day. I told him that I would be fine. But he insisted and dropped me off at my mother and stepfather's house.

I was feverish and prayed for God to give me the strength to handle her that day. As soon as my husband left, she asked me why I had come to her. Why didn't I go to my father's house and let him take care of me? She spoke in Cambodian, thus my stepdad couldn't understand what she said or comprehend why I was upset.

My father lived about a mile from her, and if I'd had the strength that day to walk to his house, I would have. My husband came over to pick me up, and I told him to never let her come near me if I am sick. Even if I was dying, she was *never* to come near me and, if she did, she was forbidden to speak Cambodian to me! I can only imagine her telling me off as I lay there dying.

She was a bitter and angry person, and I tried so hard not to become like her. In my twenties and early thirties, I was looking for a mother figure, someone to guide me, to love me, and even to cherish me. My birth mother was selfish, making everything about her. When I would get close to someone her age, my mother would try to sabotage the relationship. I wanted a mother but, ultimately, had to accept that she and I would *never* have that relationship.

I couldn't allow myself to get too close to her, or she would control and manipulate me.

Sometimes I even wondered how I would feel when she passed away. Would I feel guilty for not trying hard enough?

The truth is, even though at times, she would reach out to me, I still would not let her in. It felt like a no-win situation. I naively rationalized to myself that she would live into her seventies, giving me plenty of time to heal—and even reconcile—our relationship.

TIME AWAY

After trying to adopt and dealing with psychologists, I fell into a deep depression, and my marriage grew distant. I needed him to lean on and to be the strong one in our relationship, but he wasn't there for me emotionally. He would spend more time doing things with my single girlfriend's children. I felt hurt and betrayed by him. I felt that if I weren't barren, he would not be doing this.

I needed to find a way to start to heal within myself.

So, I got a job at a hospital in Salem, Oregon, about forty-five minutes from our vacation home. I had left him in Orange County and lived in Oregon for those nine months.

I lived up there for nine months, free from the obligations of being a dutiful wife and daughter—other than flying home to OC a couple of times on the weekends during those nine months. There were no expectations of me when I wasn't at work. It was the freedom and solitude that I needed for my healing journey to begin.

During this time, I seriously considered divorce. I didn't want to go back home. I just wanted to be free. I didn't want to live my life for anyone anymore.

But one day, my godson called and asked me to come home. So I did.

While I had been gone, my husband had developed a bitterness toward me. Our marriage was never the same when I went home.

A PROMISE

I finally gave up all hope of having my own family and still had to face more backlash. It is undoubtedly challenging to be Cambodian and barren! My mother's social circle gossiped again, asking why I couldn't have or didn't want children and speculating that it was because I had been with too many men. If I had told them that I was busy with my career and didn't want children, they would call me selfish because I need children to leave my possessions when I die.

I would try to just walk away and remind myself of what my father had said: What matters is that I know the truth, and I don't owe *anyone* an explanation.

But, alone, I would grieve for the family that I would never have. My friends were having babies and inviting me to baby showers. The pain was too much for me to handle alone, so I bared my soul to my God. One day I decided to fast and pray for His guidance, reassurance, and peace in my heart. I prayed that He would give me the heart to accept whatever He has in store for me—to accept that I may never be a mother or give me the strength to wait on His time. He put a scripture, Isaiah 54, 1-8, on my heart:

Sing, O barren woman, you who never bore a child; burst into song, shout for joy, you who were never in labor; because more are the children of the desolate woman than of her who has a husband," says the LORD. "Enlarge the place of your tent, stretch your curtains wide, do not hold back; lengthen your cords, strengthen your stakes. For you will spread out to the right and to left; your descendants will dispossess nations and settle in their desolate cities. Do not be afraid; you will not suffer shames. Do not be a disgrace; you will not be humiliated. You will forget the shame of your youth and remember no more the reproach of your widowhood. For your Maker is your husband—the LORD Almighty is His name—the Holy One of Israel is Your Redeemer; He is called the God of all the earth. The LORD will call you back as if you were a wife deserted and distressed in spirit—a wife who married young, only to be rejected," says your God. "For a brief moment, I abandoned you, but with deep compassion, I will bring you back. In a surge of anger, I hid my face from you, but with everlasting kindness, I will have compassion on you," says the LORD your Redeemer.

God was speaking to His children of Israel, but this was also His promise to me. I knew He would give me children. I didn't know how or when, but I just needed to be patient and wait on His time and not on my time.

He will know when I am truly ready.

DINNER FOR TWO

Occasionally, I would visit a bar and order dinner after work. One night I sat next to an older couple, and the three of us started talking. When she got up to leave, I realized she wasn't his wife, but a friend who co-owned the restaurant with her son.

I stayed and talked with this man in his sixties, who traveled often for work. That night he gave me a walking tour of Salem, pointing out all the good restaurants. Later that night, we went to a bar with arcade games and pinball machines. It was so fun, reminding me of times in my childhood when friends and I played those same games at the 7-Eleven.

The man and I became friends, and when he was in town for work, he'd text to see if I wanted to join him for dinner or hang out downtown. We were both foodies, and his travel for his job allowed him to stay at fancy hotels and eat at 5-star restaurants. However, he did share with me that it was a lonely life, and the reason for his failed marriage.

I was stuck in an unhappy marriage and trying to make it work, even though my husband's verbal and mental abuse drove me away from home and away from him as much as possible. I felt safer away from him. I got tired of always being beaten down and was starting to doubt myself and experiencing even lower self-esteem. I thought that I couldn't do *anything* right. I had failed at everything, especially at being a good daughter and wife.

I carried an overwhelming sense of loss and I was *really* skilled at hiding my feelings and emotions—I'd done it my whole life! I didn't open up to people, and I wasn't letting anyone in. So this new friendship, too, ended up going by the wayside,

No Changing My Mind

While I learned over time to trust and love my husband, my marriage was still falling apart. I would befriend single women with children, spend time with their children, take them out, and do things with them. My husband would grow close to the kids to the point that they would be more important to him than I was. We started arguing and fighting a lot. He would curse me out, call me names, and even called me "an evil bitch." He said I could go ahead and hide behind my Christianity all I wanted, but I was an *evil* person.

His words struck a chord with me that I will never forget. It was one thing to call me names, but it was another thing to belittle me because of my faith. He had become an angry and bitter person. He started losing his temper with his employees and even with customers. He would take the kids out behind my back, and when I confronted him about it, he would curse me out.

He was clear that he didn't want to live in California anymore. As his mood and temper grew worse, I was willing to move to the country to try to save our marriage. In January 2015, we moved to a town in Oregon that was so small there was hardly anything in it. I was isolated from my friends, and he knew it. His temper flared.

I remembered that my father made me promise to finish college and have a career so that I would never have to feel stuck or rely on anyone to take care of me and could leave when I wanted. In Oregon, I had no one to talk to, not even a pastor. Not wanting to live with my husband's anger or in that tiny town, I accepted a job in Portland and stayed there during the week.

One day he forgot the key to the house and his phone, so he broke the bedroom window to get in. He would throw a temper tantrum, and I was always to blame. He would still see me at fault, and he could *never* be wrong, so I stopped talking to him about our problems. I couldn't see the point. I wanted us to speak with our pastor, but my husband said it was all me, not him, and that I should go to counseling. I didn't know what to do. Divorce wasn't an option: I knew that was wrong. I had told myself—and had even told him—that I would only divorce him for two reasons: if he ever physically laid a hand on me or if one of us ever cheated on the other. The verbal abuse I could handle. I had been through worse.

I am cursed, I thought to myself. *I will always be abused.* I had endured my husband's verbal abuse for the past thirteen years of our marriage. I felt suffocated and trapped in a toxic marriage. Why was I still hanging on to it? Was I wanting my mother's approval and wanting to please her? Was *that* why I stayed in this miserable marriage for so long?

In 2016, he had a scheduled surgery and asked me to wake him up at 5:30 a.m. for an 8 a.m. procedure. That seemed too early, but I figured maybe he wanted to get some work done around the house because he would be down for a few days. I woke him at 5:30 a.m., and I stayed in bed.

But then he lost it on me.

Why did I wake him when he asked if I knew that he could have stayed in bed for another hour? That morning, I knew I would divorce him.

At his pre-op, he told the surgeons if he stopped breathing and if anything happened, just to let him die. I refused to talk to him all morning and was thinking to myself, *"As if any surgeon is going to let him die on the operating table!"*

I decided to stay married but distant while he recovered and waited for his tests to come back negative. Too many times, he had promised to change, only to slide back into his old ways.

I had decided to leave, and there was no changing my mind.

In Death, A New Beginning

That summer, my sister-in-law called to tell me that my mother had a stroke and was in an emergency room in Carson City, Nevada. In a second phone call, sounding more urgent, my sister-in-law told me that my mother had been outside watering plants and had been found unconscious by her driveway. Then I got a third call an hour later telling me to hurry up and get there because my mother had had a hemorrhagic stroke, and they could not operate on her. She wasn't going to make it.

I flew to Carson City, but my mother died before I got there. I had thought about this so many times and had dreaded this day. I worked as a hospice nurse and as a hospice nurse practitioner, and so many times I had wondered how I would feel if my mother passed away. Would I have any regrets or remorse? Would I feel guilty for shutting her out of my life and never letting her get close to me? I thought that I would have a decade or so to sort these feelings out. I had let her in so many times only to be hurt and let down—until I finally shut her out of my life.

To my surprise, what I felt was relief. I was free of her abuse, control, and scrutiny. The dark cloud that was hanging over me was slowly dissipating. I never had my known my identity and didn't know who I was as a person. I had to discover who I was.

For the first time, I could live for me.

TOO CLOSE

My husband's anger was getting worse. I thought perhaps it was the stress of where we lived that caused him to be angry, so in January 2015, we moved to Oregon to make our vacation home our permanent home. I hoped he would be less angry and happier not to live in a busy city. But soon enough, I came to the realization he was an angry and bitter person no matter where we lived. I took a job as far away from home as possible and rented an apartment near work during the weekdays. I would only go home on the weekends—and I dreaded it every time.

With my dinner-date friend, all conversations were light and fun, never getting too close to serious topics. And yet, I was starting to get too emotionally close to him. It scared me.

In August 2016, my husband and I attended my girlfriend's wedding. The thing about weddings is that they make you remember your own vows...

The next day I texted my foodie friend to see if he was in town and if we could talk.

Right at that moment, my husband called me and asked me what I was doing and where I was going. I told him that I was going to meet a friend. He asked if he could join us. I said no. And then—a lightbulb went off. I remembered a friend telling me that her jealous husband had put a spy application on her phone.

I was going to tell my friend that I couldn't see him anymore. But my husband's reaction showed a lack of trust that crossed a line.

When I met up with my friend, I told him that I was getting a divorce—and that I didn't want to talk about it. To cheer me up, he took me on a tour of downtown Salem again like that night when we first met.

Before this, I told my husband that I would only divorce him if he ever physically laid a hand on me or cheated on me. But, that night, I divorced him in my heart.

For the first time, I accepted my foodie friend's invitation up to his room. I had no intention of doing anything; I just didn't want to be alone that night. I was hurt, confused, and mourning the loss of my marriage.

That night I broke my marital vows, so now. My husband would now have all the excuses in the world to divorce me. The damage was done; there was no going back. Everything I thought I believed in went out the window in one night.

To top it off, I later discovered that my foodie friend was married.

Breaking Away

Right around the time of my mother's passing, my husband's lab work came back negative. I told him I wanted a divorce. *Now* he wanted us to get counseling, but I told him it was too late for that. All those years, when I asked for us to get counseling, he said to me that he didn't need it, and it was all me—so I went alone. That morning of his surgery, I had already made up my mind to divorce him. My mother had passed away, and I wanted to be free from all forms of abuse. I wanted to be happy. At forty-five-years-old, I was no longer willing to be treated as if I was worthless.

Our divorce was final at the end of September 2016.

I had to do some soul searching and figure out who I was on my own. I had lived according to my mother's rules, then my husband's, and somewhere along the way, lost my own identity. The next three years weren't easy. I was angry at everyone who had ever hurt me—and who continued to hurt me. I was getting texts from my ex-husband that I knew were actually from his new wife—her grammar was much better than his! He must have been telling lies about me to her and our mutual friends. I prayed that God would reveal the truth without me having to defend or explain myself.

I know the truth in my heart, and I know my God knows the truth. But losing friends still hurt.

God, I prayed, *please protect my heart from hatred and darkness. Please give me a heart of compassion and to love others as You have loved me. May my light never be dimmed in the darkness of this world. May your light shine through me and illuminate the paths for me to walk on in the darkness of my life.*

I became isolated as I tried to hide our divorce from the Cambodian community out of fear of judgment. I often lay in bed and stared into the darkness for hours, not wanting to get up. It took everything in me to make myself get up. I didn't want to do anything. My life was falling apart.

My closest friend, who had known my husband well, too, said that he had divorced me in his heart a long time ago, and he had been waiting for me to be the one to divorce him.

I wasn't even sure who I was without my husband.

My father had always told me that no matter how successful or how much money I have, don't ever forget my humble beginnings and the people who helped me get there.

And so I went back to the beginning.

I went to Cambodia.

HOME(LAND)

My husband had always been afraid that something would happen to me if I went back to Cambodia to help my people. But, after my divorce, I went on a church mission trip to Cambodia in October 2016. As I stepped onto my homeland for the first time, no longer a small child, I had butterflies in my stomach. I thought to myself, *"I am home. I finally made it back home."*

I wasn't sure what to expect.

Part of this trip was heartbreaking. Our mission group toured the Tuol Sleng Genocide Museum. According to BBC.com, "Tuol Sleng, codenamed S-21, was converted from a school to an interrogation center on the orders of Pol Pot when his Khmer Rouge movement took control of Cambodia in April 1975." It was the site where many educated and wealthy people were brutally killed so there would be no leaders left to retaliate. The poor and the uneducated people were left alive to do manual work and farming, and once they were no longer physically capable, they too were killed. More than 2 million Cambodians were slaughtered in less than five years.

When I had first arrived in Cambodia, I took a "tuktuk"—an auto-rickshaw—and toured Phnom Penh. The tuktuk was scary. Nobody abided by the traffic laws. Cars, motorcycles, and tuktuks were weaving everywhere, going in and out of traffic. Pedestrians ran through traffic in zigzags. There was trash everywhere. The marketplace was also dirty and crowded.

Poverty was everywhere, but especially in the villages where people lived in bamboo huts, some of them rundown or never completed, with no electricity, plumbing, or clean water. Children in rural villages often work with their families rather than go to school.

The children and the people that we helped on this trip were so grateful for what little bit that we could give them.

I saw that, no matter how bad I thought my life was, it could be worse. I thank God that I have all that I need.

It was hard to see people living in rural villages in poverty; children left home alone while their parents tried to make a living. Little children out on the streets trying to sell things to help the family. Older men and women abandoned by their children begging along the road. There were so many men with missing limbs. How could one person help all these people? The city of Phnom Penh was filthy, and there was trash everywhere. There were old European and American men with young Cambodian girls, which made me sick to my stomach. I detested those men for taking advantage of those girls. But, this was my home, my birthplace.

I thanked God that He had brought me out of that country and that I was able to provide a living for myself. Now, I thought about how to give back. While there, I fell in love with the people of Cambodia. Despite their poverty, struggles, and everything they went through during the war, they still smile. They are the friendliest people I have ever met and are so appreciative of everything.

Our church had a property called The Children's Center in the rural parts of Kampong Chhnang to provide free education for village children and dinner three times per week. School was in the evening, so the children could go to school after helping their parents work. Every Christmas, we would have a big event for all the people in the village. The Children's Center would feed everyone from around that village, a thousand people or more. During our annual mission trip, we would provide school supplies to about 1,000 children in the surrounding villages.

I see now that part of this trip was God opening a new door in my life. During this first trip to Cambodia, God put five children—my pastor's nephew's children—in my heart to adopt. Their parents were poor and did their best to provide for their family. The whole family loved God, and they had the heart to help the poor people of Cambodia. They had such loving, serving hearts. They were always there with our team helping with the cooking, cleaning, and anything else that needed to be done.

It is not uncommon in our culture to adopt children from family members, friends, or strangers. Our goal is to give a better life to our children. If we cannot afford to provide them with a better life or pay for their education, if someone comes along to offer the children an opportunity for a better life, we would release our children to that person.

I felt that God had put it in my heart that these were the children He had in mind for me. They were going to be my children, whom I could love wholeheartedly, and even better, they had their parents to take care of them when I was not there so I wouldn't have to worry about them. I wanted to be sure that it was indeed God that was putting these feelings into my heart and that I was not acting out of pure emotion. I wanted to adopt the whole family, including their parents. Their mother and father are like my younger brother and sister to me.

I prayed for guidance and asked God that if I came back next year and felt the same way about these children, I would know that this desire came from Him.

Damaged Goods—Together

Children were one thing, but my trust issues with men went much deeper. A friend recommended that I join an online dating site and go on dates for fun—nothing serious. I wasn't sure about online dating, but most of my girlfriends had met their husbands or boyfriends online. So I tried it. Every date I went on, I would imagine if I could see myself married to this man. If the answer was yes, we would go on a second date. There usually wasn't a second date.

A week before Christmas 2017, I had just returned to town from working out of town all week. I had been chatting with a man for about a week or so. We decided to meet for coffee at Starbucks in Oregon City. Meeting for coffee worked for me; it felt safe, and if I didn't feel a connection, at least we had an enjoyable conversation over a cup of coffee. When I first met him, I thought, "Wow, is this too good to be true? He is tall, quite good looking, and intelligent. Our conversation was quite stimulating. He loved rocks as much as I did, and it turned out we both had quite a collection of stones.

To my roommate's surprise, I did go on a second date.

This man had a son, who I met. He wasn't hiding anything from me. Regardless, I still felt weirded out, trapped, and insecure, like I was riding an emotional roller coaster. And there was my discomfort with being in an intimate relationship outside of marriage. I would try to end the relationship every couple of months. But he would give me my space when I needed space or be there for me when I needed a shoulder to cry on. There seemed to be nothing I could do to push him away. He, too, had issues he was working through, and I would be there for him emotionally.

We were damaged goods—together.

But sex outside of marriage was a heavy burden in my heart. He knew that and never tried to cross that line. So, after a year of breaking up in cycles, we decided to be just friends. Best friends who cuddle, but don't have sex.

From then on, every time I've gone on a date, I've had to share with the date that my best friend is my ex-boyfriend and that my other best friend is my male roommate. If there's a problem with that, there's no second date. I won't choose.

My friends joke that if I stopped being so picky, I would find the right guy. But I will not compromise anymore. I've learned from the past, and I know what I want in a relationship: A man who loves and walks with God. A man of strong faith and integrity who has a serving heart. A man who will honor me, respect me, and love me unconditionally as Christ loves him. It's hard, but I am going to stand firm in my faith and my belief. God has that special man out there for me, and I pray that God will work on both of us. Or, if I am meant to be alone, I know God will prepare my heart for that. I trust that all is in divine order.

Phnom Penh

It's my second trip back home to Cambodia.

I woke up early this morning at 4:30 a.m. my time. I thought I'd go walking before everyone woke up, but Phnom Penh is already awake.

As I walk through the open market, merchants are busy cleaning and chopping meat, setting out their merchandise, and preparing food. Mopeds, motorcycles, and tuktuks are everywhere as people make deliveries. The air smells of pickled mudfish, meat, and seafood mixed with the fumes of exhaust from mopeds, cars, motorcyclists, and tuktuks.

Vendors are bustling to set out their food carts along the waterfront, cooking for the day's water festival. Here, I smell saltwater and lemongrass and spices. I watch the sunrise over the Mekong River with beautiful colors.

On the opposite side, the view is different: The sidewalks are crowded with vendors, and trash blankets the sidewalks, which smell of urine. I also see other groups of people doing their morning exercises. Walking, dancing to hip hop music, or doing tai chi to traditional Cambodian Chinese instrumentals.

Walking into the tourist neighborhood, I see merchants are busily sweeping the sidewalks in front of their stores. Foreigners, mostly Europeans, sip freshly brewed coffee and nibble on pastries as they people-watch.

This city awakens all the senses. I am open and see, hear, smell, touch, and taste all of what she has to offer. This city had endured much, if you know her history, but is now thriving and emanating the beauty that she once was.

A Promise Fulfilled

At the end of my second trip to Cambodia in 2017, I asked to speak to my pastor and his wife alone. "*A decade ago, God had given me scriptures that I held onto,*" I told them, "*and the scriptures were a promise to give me children,*" I said to them that I always knew I would be coming back home to Cambodia to serve our people, but that God had also put these five children in my heart. I shared how I felt about them the previous year and how I still felt the same way and knew it was from God.

I told them that I wanted to adopt the whole family—including the parents.

The evening before I was supposed to leave to come back to the States, we called for a meeting with my pastor, his wife, the elders from the church, his nephew's family, and me. It was the next step for discussing how I could be a part of the children's life.

I told the children that I would adopt them under one condition—that they promise when they grew up and became successful that they would do something for another child living in poverty, perhaps even adopting and paying for that child's education, too.

I shared my truth. I was a stranger who was willing to adopt and provide for the whole family and pay for all their education. I asked that they remember the kindness that was shown to them and pay it forward. They all agreed, so I adopted them and have never looked back or regretted it. God was working with me.

God gave me a sense of purpose.

I am no longer living for me. I now have these beautiful children—children who I always dreamed of having—to live for and to provide for.

For the next year or so, these kids kept me out of my depression. I woke up every morning and went to work, so I could live up to my promise to them and make sure they were taken care of. They became my reason for living.

Searching for Meaning in All the Wrong Faces

With my divorce, I had lost my identity and had to find myself again. It was not a comfortable journey. My children had saved me because no matter how depressed or how down a dark road I had walked, I knew that they needed me.

I knew what I wanted in a relationship and what I was looking for with a partner. Once again, I had to throw everything I believed in out the window—just like I had when I was in the military. Marriage was not sacred to me anymore; it was merely a piece of paper that had caused pain and suffering. I'd been married to a Christian man for twenty-three years, and he treated me terribly, so I had developed a hatred toward Christian men and chose to stay away from them.

I dated one man who became my best friend, and then I pushed him out of my life. I would get close to him, then push him away. I wanted to be in a relationship... and then I didn't. I was always looking for an escape route. Within one year of dating, I had broken up with him at least six times. Yet he remained a close friend. He even contributed to the cost of my mission trip in 2017.

My next dating relationship was similar.

Within three years after my divorce, I still couldn't commit to any relationship. I would get close, get scared, and push them away. I wanted companionship and someone to do things with. But I was afraid of being hurt or disappointed. I was at my weakest at night when my worries and emotions would take over. I dated all the wrong men. God had put it in my heart that I needed to be with someone equally yoked, and yet I kept dating men who didn't believe in God. Perhaps that was part of why I would sabotage every relationship.

I felt convicted with my choice of lifestyle. Even while dating nonbelievers, I would ask God to please help me with my loneliness and the void inside me. I wanted to be loved but had never experienced it. I loved my godchildren, my niece and nephews, and my children. But in a romantic relationship, I have never loved anyone. My ex-husband and I stayed married as long as we did out of duty and obligation.

I knew that God hated divorce, so I stayed in a loveless marriage because of my faith—and because I didn't want to fail. I didn't want my mother to be right that I was worthless and not good at anything. I had lived my whole life to prove her wrong, and when she passed away, all that weight I was carrying was lifted off my shoulders. I felt free to do what I wanted and live my own life as the authentic me. I never wanted to get married in the first place, but I had done it out of duty to my mother.

Being in one meaningless relationship after another was eating away at my very core. Finally, one day in September 2019, I realized I was done. I didn't like men. To me, Christian and non-Christian men were all the same. They all had the same thing in mind. I was no different from them. God had put it in my heart that I needed to clean out my life. He had someone out there for me, but I would never meet him if I continued with my ungodly lifestyle. A friend had loaned me a book called "Finding Your Million Dollar Soul Mate" by Randy Pope. That book had been sitting on top of my dresser drawer for almost a year before I finally sat down and read the whole book in one sitting.

As I read this book, I realized that I had *never* been in a healthy relationship. I had never trusted or opened up to anyone. My life, marriage, and dating relationships had always been dysfunctional. I didn't know what a normal relationship was or if I was even capable of being in one!

For my whole life, I had been closed up and shut off—never letting anyone get close enough to see me as a whole and complete person, someone with past hurts and disappointments—someone who wanted to love and be loved. I wanted someone to accept me for who I was with all my flaws.

After reading that book, I realized that what *I* wanted was what *God* had always wanted for me. Deep down, I knew that before I could have that perfect, unconditional love, I had to let go of my anger and depression.

But how? I would not seek professional counseling this time—it just hadn't gone well for me in the past.

Cleaning Up My Life

I wanted to clean up my life. I looked back at my past as a child and wondered how I had managed to overcome all of the horrors.

It was because I always prayed and never wandered far from my God. The darker my world got, the tighter clung to my God.

Even though I thought I could handle it alone, my anger and depression worsened. I was so resentful of people who had hurt me. I resented my mother, my step-grandfather, and my ex-husband.

What had I done as a child? I had to go back to that little girl. That little girl who hid in the hallway closet for hours to hide from her mother, who had constant dreams of being locked in a white room and couldn't get out, who had plans of running away in the dark, hiding in the bushes so her mother couldn't find her, that little girl who had a strong will to live, to succeed, and who was chasing that dream of having a better life for herself.

In the past, on nights when I was alone and feeling angry or depressed with my emotions all over the place, I would call or text one of my closest friends, who were both ex-boyfriends, and just entangle myself and cause chaos with them.

But now I chose not to do that. I fought the urge to pick up the phone. I cried and pleaded with God to help me. I prayed, listened to Christian music, and read my Bible. Anytime I felt any negative emotions or had any negative thoughts, I would pray and read scripture. If I were driving, I would pray and listen to my Christian music.

I was determined to change my life for the better.

Mission Field

In November 2019, I went on my third mission trip to Cambodia. This time we teamed up with a medical mission team from Florida, and I put my professional skills to use by providing medical care for those in need.

My two oldest adopted daughters went with me, and I did my best to give medical advice and treat symptoms with what we had. Since that trip, I've dreamed of opening a clinic that provides free medical care for those in need. I don't know how or when this will happen, but I believe that if it is meant to be, God will open the doors when the time is right.

My daughters got some exposure to the medical field, and I was grateful to train them myself. I wanted them to be successful, no matter which career they chose. I had promised myself that if I ever did have children, I would guide them as much as possible.

My oldest daughter was afraid to tell me that she didn't want to be a doctor because she couldn't handle the sight of blood. She didn't want to disappoint me, but she finally told me that she was interested in a career in information technology. I told her that I only wanted her to be happy, and if she wanted to be in IT, I would support her. She applied for an IT school in Phnom Penh and was accepted into the program.

My second oldest daughter truly excelled when we were providing medical care in rural villages. I hope she finds her calling there, and I'll support whichever direction she chooses.

Looking back, I see that God has provided me with children—my godsons, my niece and nephews, and my adopted children—to open up my heart.

Each time I have gone to Cambodia, I have come back hopeful and ready to take on what life throws at me. I am reminded that I am Cambodian, and I can overcome anything. My people are resilient. Cambodia runs deep in my veins; it is the very essence of me. The will to survive to live has always been with me. I am determined.

Whatever my future holds, I am strong enough. And I'm not alone.

<hr />

I knew that I needed someone I could trust to help me get through all the pain and past trauma. I didn't want to see a psychologist again, so I prayed and asked God to help me find someone who would understand me. I was ready to deal with my past, heal from it, and move forward in a positive direction with my life. I didn't want to be angry, depressed, or lonely. I didn't want to have to be either a whirlwind of emotions or feel nothing and in a void.

One day I had an a-ha moment, *"I should hire a life coach!"*

I found her among my Facebook friends. Reaching out to her was the beginning of my healing journey—steps forward to heal myself from past pains and trauma, truly forgive and let go, find myself, and be content with who I truly am without any masks.

PURPOSE

Sometimes a certain patient touches my heart. This morning I saw a patient who is feeling lonely, depressed, and isolated. He can't open up to his family because of fear of judgment. All his friends are either in jail or have died. He admitted that he has thoughts of killing himself but says that he would never do it.

I prayed to God, asking for wisdom on how to help this man. I asked my patient if he prays. *Yes,* he said, *but God doesn't listen to me.*

"We all feel that way sometimes," I told him. "But God is listening. We don't hear Him because we are so overwhelmed with our life and all our problems that we don't take the time to hear Him."

I admitted that sometimes I, too, am lonely, depressed and isolated. Sometimes I, too, think that I have nothing to live for. But I do. And so does he. *Every morning,* I told him, *find something to be grateful for.* A job. A place to live. Food to eat. Anything. I had to learn to do that.

I had to wake up every morning and make a conscious decision that today I am going to be grateful for something which gave me a sense of purpose.

I also told him to make a short goal for himself and that whenever he feels that he wants "to use" to remember his goal. And to think about whether "using" would destroy his goal.

I had to learn to do that—to take a moment to examine my impulses and, over time, retrain my thoughts.

Keep hope, I told him. *Always have hope.* Hope was the light into my dark soul and I would never let that light grew dim. Hang on to that hope, I told him, because in our darkest hours, it is that hope that will lift us up and out back into the light.

FORGIVENESS

My patients have shown me what holding on to the past, not letting go, and not forgiving those who have hurt you can do to a person. It leads to self-destruction. Some of my patients have lost everything—jobs, families, homes, even their self-worth—as they held onto those past hurts. I see how it consumes them.

I realized that I needed to do a lot of forgiving.

How do I forgive? I thought of my God. He had never hurt anyone and yet He was crucified on the cross. Even while on the cross, He forgave. And, though I have failed Him again and again, He has never given up on me.

So, who am I to hold a grudge?

I remembered a pastor once saying to me, "If you hate someone, pray for them because it is impossible to hate the person you prayed for."

Every night I prayed for them—my mother and father, my ex-husbands, and even my step-grandfather. At first, I dredged up memories. But I sorted through them and kept praying. Then slowly, my heart softened. And when I thought about them, instead of feeling hatred and anger, I felt sadness that they were broken, too.

My life coach suggested that I write. I started writing, and all those memories I had suppressed for decades came bubbling to the surface.

Finally, I understood the source of all those negative feelings and emotions I was experiencing.

I am letting it all go. All my past traumas, pain, hurt, disappointment, and betrayal—they are no longer for me to keep. I release them all and I give it to God for He will carry all my burdens.

I forgive my mother for abusing me, my step-grandfather for sexually molesting me, my father for not shielding me, and my ex-husband for not seeing me, valuing me, or putting me first.

I forgive them, just as God has forgiven me my sins.

TWO RINGS

Two nights ago, I had a dream about that first intimate relationship after my marriage. The man who had hidden from me that he was married—as I was, too, when we first met.

In the dream, he knelt and held a ring that was tied to another ring. The ring band was rose color with a pink rectangular stone with an off-white overlay of a vine on the right corner of the stone. From this ring dangled another smaller ring with two little diamonds that was not of great clarity or color. I could see the flaws in those two little diamonds.

He held the ring out to me, and I put it on my left fourth finger. The first ring was a ring of forgiveness, and the attached ring was a promise ring that he would marry me someday— but I wasn't sure if that was what I wanted.

I remembered the times when I had laid alone at night crying because I couldn't understand why we couldn't talk on the phone, text more often, or even spend the weekends together. Then to find out that he was married and that I had been deceived... I felt that I had to end the relationship and close that chapter of my life.

I needed to forgive him. And forgive myself.

And then in my dream, as I held both rings, I gently slid only that first ring of forgiveness onto my finger.

CALLING

Forgiveness is powerful. I would not change anything that happened to me or what I went through because my life experience gave me a purpose. It gave me the will to survive and to succeed. It gave me a compassionate heart to reach out to those who are hurting with an understanding of what they are going through because I went through it myself. It made my relationship with my God stronger because He was always there for me.

I have found my calling. Today, I work with people who are lost, depressed, isolated, and feel that they are worthless. Whatever past traumas, shame, guilt, feelings, thoughts, or emotions my patients tell me they are going through, I know it all too well. I have the opportunity to help them navigate through it and be a part of their life for that one visit. That one visit I get to give them hope, and help them to see that life is beautiful, they have a purpose, and that no matter how they may feel, they are loved.

It took forty-nine years for me to get here. I finally came to a place where I have happiness, true contentment, and peace. I am okay being alone. Now in the silence of the night I feel safe and emotionally sound. My void has been filled with the love of my God, my children, and my niece and nephews. Though I am barren, God had surrounded me with children. Though I was broken, He picked up all my broken pieces and glued me back together until I was made whole again in His image.

I will not let myself linger in dark places anymore. I will find sunlight deep in my soul, and will find a way to always let it shine. I will feel the warmth of the sun's rays on my face again. Because I am worth loving.

Acknowledgments

I thank my beautiful friend and life coach, Alis Mao, who inspired and encouraged me to start a journal. My writing brought a flood of emotions to the surface, but then she was there for me to sort out my anger, shame, guilt, regrets, depression, loneliness, and anxiety. Over several months of writing and processing emotions, I came to realize that I no longer felt dirty or ashamed or guilt. In fact, for the first time I felt the way I had always wanted to feel: normal. Having gone through all that pain, shame, embarrassment, and self-doubt and come out the other side, I feel equipped to be in service to others though my sacred work in the world.

I also want to thank Donna Templin who was like a mother to me when I was a teenager. When I was homeless and had no where to go she took me in and loved me like a daughter. I had never forgotten her kindness towards me. She was always proud of me and told me if I was her daughter she would be so proud of me.

I want to thank my Dad. He was the stable one in my life. Taught me to be independent in his own way. I miss him everyday and I hope he is proud of me now as he always was.

I want to thank my mother, too. She didn't know that her abuse made me the person I am today: strong, independent, resilient, kind, loving, and compassionate.

Most importantly I want to thank my Lord Jesus Christ. He was always there for me and never left my side. I didn't see it then, but I see it now and I am grateful.

ABOUT THE AUTHOR

Rina Liv, APRN is a traveling nurse practitioner working in the field of addiction medicine. Having endured a lifetime of physical, sexual, and emotional abuse in silence, her sacred work is to share hope with others who have suffered from abuse and turned to drugs or alcohol to numb their pain or forget their past.

Rina's dream is to show and spread God's love by opening a medical clinic in her birth country of Cambodia, providing free medical care for those in need. In partnership with fellow Flower of Life Press author Alis Mao, Rina intends to make this dream a reality and help the people of Cambodia, many of whom continue to suffer from the genocide that was experienced in the 1970's.

While on a mission trip to Cambodia, Rina fell in love with five children, whom she adopted a year later and has vowed to love and support as her own. She provides financial support and visits Cambodia as much as possible to share in their lives. Her oldest daughter, in college, is majoring in IT information technology. Her second oldest daughter plans to attend college and become a designer.

Despite her painful past, Rina is optimistic about love! She trusts that a man of strong faith who loves God and who has a heart to serve others will find his way into her life. A foodie at heart, she enjoys going to restaurants, cooking, and entertaining friends. She lives in Oregon and enjoys hiking, traveling, and visiting wineries. Rina began writing as part of her healing journey, and is currently working on her second book, *Disillusioned Love*.

Traveling the Road of Solitude

·····⊶⊷·····

Additional books by Flower of Life Press

The New Feminine Evolutionary: Embody Presence—Become the Change

Pioneering the Path to Prosperity: Discover the Power of True Wealth and Abundance

Sacred Body Wisdom: Igniting the Flame of Our Divine Humanity

Set Sail: Shine Your Radiance, Activate Your Ascension, Ignite Your Income, Live Your Legacy

Practice: Wisdom from the Downward Dog

Sisterhood of the Mindful Goddess: How to Remove Obstacles, Activate Your Gifts, and Become Your Own Superhero

Path of the Priestess: Discover Your Divine Purpose

Sacred Call of the Ancient Priestess: Birthing a New Feminine Archetype

Rise Above: Free Your Mind One Brushstroke at a Time

Menopause Mavens: Master the Mystery of Menopause

The Power of Essential Oils: Create Positive Transformation in Your Well-Being, Business, and Life

Self-Made Wellionaire: Get Off Your Ass(et), Reclaim Your Health, and Feel Like a Million Bucks

Emerge: 7 Steps to Transformation (No matter what life throws at you!)

Oms From the Mat: Breathe, Move, and Awaken to the Power of Yoga

Oms From the Heart: Open Your Heart to the Power of Yoga

The Four Tenets of Love: Open, Activate, and Inspire Your Life's Path

The Fire-Driven Life: Ignite the Fire of Self-Worth, Health, and Happiness with a Plant-Based Diet

Becoming Enough: A Heroine's Journey to the Already Perfect Self

The Caregiving Journey: Information. Guidance. Inspiration.

Plant-based Vegan & Gluten-free Cooking with Essential Oils

www.floweroflifepress.com

FREE Mini-Course: www.bestsellerpriestess.com/bestseller-priestess